POST COLONIAL
IDENTITIES

-

Smith and Ce [ed.]

AFRICAN

Library of Critical Writing

POST COLONIAL IDENTITIES
Smith and Ce (Ed.)

©African Library of Critical Writing
Print Edition
ISBN: 978-9-7837-0857-0

For information address:
Progeny (Press) International
Email: progeny.int@gmail.com
For: African Books Network
9 Handel Str.
AI EBS Nigeria WA
Email: handelbook@gmail.com

Marketing and Distribution in the US, UK,
Europe, N. America (Canada),
and Commonwealth countries by

African Books Collective Ltd.
PO Box 721
Oxford OX1 9EN
United Kingdom
Email: orders@africanbookscollective.com

Contents

Editors' Note

POST Colonial Identities revisits issues regarding the new literatures within a heritage of diverse regional and national groupings. It is poised at substantiating the uniformity of Africa in terms of literary and cultural movements, and lending some inter-disciplinary insights on that whole body of literature through the complex progress of twentieth century history. In the words of one contributor, 'recognizing such complexity of Black cultures will help us better understand the cultural, economic, and political relationships between Blacks of Africa and of the Diaspora.'

An exemplar of imaginative critical evaluation comes in the 'eclectic approach' to new oeuvres which, with the inclusivity of exclusive forms (poetry and fiction) as one whole movement of 'dialogue,' 'transition' and 'memory,' adds an important dimension to understanding the new voices from Africa.

We have excerpted two post-colonial discourses that would fascinate many college departments of African literature. Both readings beat the *Fall Apart* track with an interesting sidebar coming at the point where that principal African fiction is set against the younger novels. Also readers may find the reading of *Things Fall Apart* and *Macbeth* problematic in the branding of superstition on belief and culture systems not entirely in conformity with Christian motifs. But this does not invalidate the comparative relevance and the higher concerns of the work.

The counterpoint of this work comes up in the entries which differ in their opinions of the vision and craft of two postcolonial writers of Indian and African ethnicities. While we might seem empathetic with Mongo Beti's artistic

5

limitations in *Mission Terminie* (*Mission to Kala*) and argue that the alienation of the hero in both narrative and action serves a satiric purpose that bears upon an essentially colonial precedent, we seem to spare little regard for Naipaul's 'thwarted' vision of history and struggle through *A House*. Likewise there is disdain upon claims of Wole Soyinka's indebtedness to Brecht in *The Swamp Dwellers* with spirited arguments that in spite of the play's obvious imitation of *Waiting for Godot*, both works, mythically interpreted, tap from a collective mythic imagination.

We have an insight on the new treatment of male characters in fiction, perhaps, in keeping with a Feminist reading of literature. Added with the very original study of masculinity in Ghanaian stories both entries propose a valid complement in developing the artistic historiography of the Ghanaian nation state.

Coetzee's *Disgrace* has been dubbed a work of 'existentialist maturation.' The chapter is important in the two ways with which it gently knocks the pedestrianism of Swales and Savran while offering a mildly coterminous but distinctive approach to that peculiar novel. Our review of the problems of African modernity in relation to Gilroy's 'Black Atlantic' definitely makes an impressive finale for the series. And with the reviews of the Anezi Okoro's novel, *The Flying Tortoise*, and Judith Coullie's women's life writing, *The Closest of Strangers*, in addition to Bettina Weiss' contemporary perspectives on Southern African literatures, *The End of Unheard Narratives*, we conclude our third library of critical approaches to African literature.

While expressing our gratitude to all our contributors for their hard work and patience through the arduous process of putting this edition together, we should add that our success would have been wholly impossible without the assistance of the collegiate board. Very many thanks therefore to the continued patronage of Africa Research International which has singularly prepared the stage for our world network of contributors to chart Africa's literary creeks in sister volumes. -*CS and CC*

Chapter One

Dialogue and Transition in Recent Oeuvres

A.Grants

Tenors of Transition in *An African Eclipse*

BEGINNING with *An African Eclipse* (AE) Chin Ce's oeuvres foreshadow a general communal retardation most poignant in the *Koloko* and *Gamji* fictions[1]. Seen together as one movement, these writings trace a movement in the major characters from one of social preoccupation to that of psychological transition in awareness and growth.

'A Farewell' (AE) highlights this movement in a prefatory manner. The three ways: left, right and middle signify three choices involving two extremes and a middle course, an important element in Ce's oeuvres. Before the choice is made, the characters must face their fears and actions represented in 'only our own graffiti.' The choice of a middle alternative is imperative from the flagellation of the other extremities but it is a lonely route that marks a separation from friends, old values, and life ways. In *Children of Koloko*, Yoyo represents this third factor and his separation from his two friends, Dickie and Buff, finally marks his attainment of growth as we shall see later.

With the choice enacted in full awareness of the sense of alienation engendered, progress is sure even if the social

8

outcome of this progress in political and social discourse may be uncertain.

'May 29 1999', a historical poem on the inauguration of Nigeria's last democracy confronts us with the grotesque physical paunch and slovenliness of Nigeria's new civilian leadership which combine with poetic epithets to forecast political disaster. 'The curse of the triangle' is another slavery which the new government portends for the generality of the Nigerian people. This cynicism has been justified in the society-evident lack of direction that rated that country one of the most corrupt nations on earth under the new government. It is the fraud of nation building which Africa's postcolonial founding fathers had mistaken for patriotism. Its impact on the younger generations to come is being witnessed in contemporary politics of attrition and dislocation of previously honoured traditional values, a situation that was forewarned in the second fiction *Gamji College*.

'Second Cousin' continues the dialogue of the younger generation which crystallizing in Ce's prose fiction *Children of Koloko*. The Nigerian youth such as 'Hugo, the burly head of the thuggery squad' (*Koloko* 79) has metamorphosed in his 'gold and bangle epaulettes' as the 'success' story of Nigeria's upper social class even with odd jobs to his credit. His sponsors are men who, with the combination of politically motivated murders, extortion, bribery, and corruption have become governors of states or chairs of local municipal councils. The nation is consequently in deep political, social, and economic trouble with such fraudulence among the high and low.

'Wind and Storm' furthers the dialogue on the trouble with Nigeria from Achebe's published position on a similar subject. In this discourse, the poet avers that self-inflicted wounds are no machination of destiny, especially for such a prayerful community which Nigeria with its deepening Muslim-Christian divide. The consequences of this malady ('stoked by touts at Government House(s)') are myriad. Environmental degradation ('craters of the Niger') is a corollary of government neglect and paucity of imaginative thinking. ('There are no sages on silent feet.') Where the instance of leadership exists, there abounds an overstock of quasi-scholarship and religious zealotry.

'The Preacher' satirises a religious environment of pew sanctimony and its failing impact on the sensitivity of the young ones. The timeworn and consequently unimaginative religious dialogue 'let him hear who has ears' begs effective communication with frenzied gestures ('in the crescendo of agitation'). Since the sermon degenerates to boredom and 'consecrated tedium,' imagination must be given free vent in escape from the stifling environment of religious extravaganzas.

The poet's delineated 'eclipse' is therefore of a postcolonial transition that can only be determined by the quality of both leadership and citizenship in contemporary African republics. The evidence of internal social contradictions and ungainly stirring in the form of political upheavals within the continent naturally justifies the cynicism with which a poet and writer like Chin Ce would draw us to the centre of the African pedagogy.

Song, Drama, and Memory in *Children of Koloko*

Children of Koloko marks out at initial reading as something of a childhood story of innocence. But it really isn't. What we have are character types seen through the central character, Yoyo, and other bohemian adjuncts of the central personage mainly Dickie and Buff.

So we have three youngsters who are negotiating their passage into adulthood and are keenly aware of the deficiencies of their environment –and of themselves. These are therefore some kind of social critics but not in an aloof, self-righteous manner. They are all participants in a drama of social transition and psychological awareness. The result is a kind of growth. But while the society records painful imperviousness to change, the pace of psychological growth of the hero predictably outmatches all of his contemporaries.

Yoyo is a kind of interrogator engaged in dialogue with society. The first part of the story introduces him as a precocious child prodigy. His imagination is definitely and highly spectroscopic.

> Heaven's clouds rolled in a beautiful surging mass of flaming blue tongues.
> …
> The clouds seemed to surge with greater momentum. Something must be happening too in the ethers, I believed. Each darting tongue of cloud was a bubble of energy flowing in space. I saw them as warriors charging on to battle against Lucifer and his own queer band of angels. I could see how they adorned themselves in grotesque sizes and shapes that kept changing and twisting and bending, now parting, then coming together to become coupled like Siamese cats. I watched calmly as they disappeared behind the veil into the unknown where the band of good angels must be standing on guard. What further threat assailed them by devil's advocates plotting to overthrow heaven and rule? (COK 17)

Coming home was, for him, an exile of a hopefully temporary
nature.

The journey was not my idea of a picnic, right from when Mam, Bap and Dora began to make preparations for our departure till we all bundled our bulks into the loaded vehicle. Not that I do not like changes as Bap did, for isn't all life full of change, as he would say. For me Boko was the only memorable event like any other place where one had grown up and got used to. So Boko had been home, if home was the house you lived and the community you had grown in, attending school each morning and picking up your habits for over fifteen years until suddenly they said a new state was born and we had become strangers there.(24)

But he adjusts quickly to his new environment thanks to two friends he had quickly taken to and who provide him with fillers in his awareness and understanding of his new environment.

'I am Dickie.'
'And this is Buff,' they introduced in the manner of another dress rehearsal.
'People used to think we are twins,' Dickie said, 'and this loafer, Buff, is always flattered,' he teased.
They must be such fine clowns, I concluded.
Dickie was a gaunt fellow with high cheekbones and wan smile that disguised his good sense of drama. But Buff was a podgy guy who would never look strict or serious with anything even from a distance.
'Let's go and spend some time at De Mica's palm wine bar at the town square,' Buff proffered. 'I'll pay.' (29-30)

Through Dickie and Buff, Yoyo soon learns a great deal about the backwardness and homelessness situation of this new neighbourhood called Koloko.

'Do you really believe that Dogkiller has seventeen wives and, over thirty-five sons and daughters' I asked Buff who only gave me a mysterious snort without an answer.

'Dickie, could this be true?' I protested. 'I mean how does he manage them?'

Dickie loudly snorted too and whispered, 'How can I tell? I've never been near his New Heaven mansion.'

'I have,' quipped Buff.... 'Such lavish edifice. Greater than any one ten of the chiefs' put together. And as large as heaven too...' (21)

Yoyo dilates quite understandably between outright rejection of the generation of his fathers and leaders such as Dogomutun and Fathead and the vicarious enjoyment of the spoils of national plunder seen in his participation in Fathead's 'house warming' ceremony. Later in 'News' we see him defending the public ridicule of his society which the likes of chief Dogkiller, the politician, had visited on it by his misappropriations of public resources.

The quality of dramatic short fiction in *Children of Koloko* comes with its spontaneity of progression via discourse --a salient, unique quality in the writing as in 'The Bottle' (GC 2001). This interaction of dialogue and songs serves to convey deep social entrenchments such as the public song at Chief Fathead's house warming ceremony:

When we eat, when we drink
Food, wine in steady flow
Do not guess O do not wonder
It's better life for rural hunger (129)

Fathead's speech at this celebration reflects the confidence tricks of the privileged elite class and the false logic of those who admire them and aspire to similar material accomplishments without the basic corollary of intellectual discernment. 'Koloko mma mma o! I salute you all. Our elders say that gbata gbata is a language that has two faces. It might mean good, it might mean disaster.' (98) In this drama of social and communal acquiescence, tradition is made culprit, a situation heightened by Fathead's use of local wisdom in two proverbs, one being that 'gbata gbata is a language that has two faces; it might mean good, it might mean disaster' and the other asserting rather hypocritically 'it is from the home front that all training must take off...' with the English equivalent of 'charity begins at home...' Of course these are mere cheap rigmarole. The women folk who applaud him are unlike their modern enlightened liberated folks who acquiesce to the impoverishment of their nation state so long as it carves for them a niche of the social table. We may later see some rising assertions in the younger generation represented by Tina and her mother, but only briefly.

The Koloko women of Fathead's generation, through their songs and dances, are active connivers in a degenerating social order. Their songs betray the subversion of art for mere toadying for personal indulgence. To support Fathead's self-dominant dialogue, the women improvise a song from an Anglican hymn. We are shown an admixture of spiritual irreverence from poor syncretism of traditional and Christian religious worship:

The millionaire cometh!
See the millionaire cometh!
All eyes have seen him and
They say the millionaire cometh!!! (133)

Both cases, particularly the latter, are inversions of their intended meaning. With communal epithets and witticism, Fathead justifies extravagant lifestyles and social ceremony -

14

actions that are the bane of real progress. The society applauds in another intent: as long as they are participants of the crumbs of the table. In their haste to satisfy their palate, even custom can be thrown overboard. 'Now how do we begin?' Mika asked. 'A hungry man does not waste the time on proverbs when the real meal is before him. De Tom what do you say?' (133). In the social dramatic, cheap and vulgar wit interact freely.

> 'Hey be careful how you cut the meat... like you don't have any bone in your wrist. See...see that one.'
> ...
> 'Whose name does he bear?' someone followed.
> 'Don't you mind these young boys of the end age.'
> 'No manhood in between, and no bones.'
> 'It's too much mischief with the girls.'
> 'Ha! Ha! Ha! (134)

Surely, Koloko is a sinking ship for the degeneracy of any society is assured when it never questions but accepts all that is thrown at it with its craving for indulgence -much like our contemporary American culture. And this is the dramatic thrust of Chin Ce's narrative: the bane of the children of Koloko (read Africa).

Transition and Dialogue in *Gamji College*

Gamji College (GC) begins on a staccato rhythm (GC 2) showcasing the dubious morality of the religions imported into Africa and embraced by an overwhelmed, uninformed and ignorant multitude. The story begins with a freshman's experience on his first day at school. Tai on arrival is beset by a proselyte band whose interest in his welfare is mere

15

pretension. It strikes the new comer that the new friends foisting themselves on him are like the local politicians represented by president Baba Sonja who do not keep their words.

> James was not quite true to his words, Tai noted with a sense of disrelish. He had come at just half past six while the arrangement was for seven. Tai was just preparing to go for dinner with another roommate called Pablo. Pablo had just checked in a few minutes ago. He was in his second year and they were just beginning to make friends. To James Tai said, 'Oh you're here,' and he tried to avoid a grimace, managing a wan smile instead.
> 'Yes, I can see you are ready.'
> Whoever said he was ready? Tai hadn't said anything to that effect...(GC 11)

The final dismissal of these unwanted elements is also the rejection of the politics of impoverishment and deceit represented in the persons of college rector Dr. Jeze and his uncle the 'born-again' president Baba Sonja. More importantly the imported religion is equally thrown aboard.

> "You must experience God!" James warned, his
> desperation sounded like a drowning man's last momentous effort to hold on to a straw.
> "And who is to give me the experience?" Tai snorted with derision, "Brother Rimi?" he laughed mirthlessly. "Or Leader Obu? Oh, what of President Sonja and his ugly paunch? Now gentlemen, James and Rock-of- Peter or is it Peter-the-Rock? Please leave me. You are really being a nuisance interrupting my sleep," he pointed gently to the door. (34)

In 'The Bottle' the second part of *Gamji College* fiction, we are not deceived by the rowdy boisterous company that Dogo,

16

Femi and Milord (which in Koloko may also read Yoyo, Dickie and Buff). The tripartite characters are metonymical of the tripod on which the Nigerian nation is said to rest, representing the three major ethnicities that had dominated the country's political scene since independence to no apparent benefit. However, the three part characters here also present a three way resolution of the past present and future more clearly illustrated in *The Visitor*, Ce's third work of fiction.

The entire racy banters suggest the juvenile delinquency of the Nigerian youth on the surface. Underneath there are currents of restiveness seen later in current threats to the nation's corporate existence by youths of the Niger Delta. The novelist clearly foresees this restiveness in the queries and exchanges of Dogo, Milord and Femi.

> 'Until you are carried back in a stretcher,' Milord retorted.
> 'Of course, what better VIP treatment? And I won't miss the sirens. No governor in this country ever rides the streets of the town without sirens.'
> 'I can get you one,' Dogo offered, 'the noisiest siren the bloodiest dictator never had.'
> 'Great then that's the making of a president. One secret pals, those guys are drunk or doped all the time. That's their courage to face the crowd…with all those lies.'
> 'And to sneak out at night to see their girlfriends…'
> 'And their harem,' Milord peered at Dogo.
> 'Talk about harem.' (55)

The youths had long lost faith in the leadership which offers nothing but self aggrandisement and self indulgence. Similarly they, lacking a credible model, offer no reliable alternative as events following the campus elections clearly testify. Napoleon, late entrant for Gamji College union presidency, is part of the thuggery and rigging that characterise

17

local elections. Napoleon proposes an incredibly reactionary political alternative:

> 'You take one step back to make two steps forward. Being a neutral for once is like that, but in this case, I manipulate it to divert the votes to me. I win, and it is victory for the revolution. Actually my comrade Yusuf derailed when he allowed his tribesmen to hijack his manifesto and that's when I decided to come in... Just come and see me deliver my manifesto,' he boasted.
> 'And if you fail?'
> 'Never,' Napoleon spat. 'No politician ever contemplates failure in this business. I'm already the chief executive of Gamji union government, and if all fails,' he made one deft movement of his right hand behind his back and fished out a pistol. 'This doesn't.' (82)

His reliance on his gun as a last alternative to fetch him victory is like the morality of successive national elections in the country which has been to rule by any means necessary and die in office. It comes as no surprise that the union elections like all Nigerian elections end in chaos and violence. The only real candidate whose manifesto appears to make sense is killed presumably by Napoleons' gun.

Return of the Prodigal in *Children of Koloko*

Again we must return to the first novel *Children of Koloko* to complete the metamorphosis of consciousness in a transitional society. In 'Return to Koloko,' Yoyo confesses earnestly,

> 'Six years and I was now a man. My CV was quite impressive. I had finished college, did a stint of press work, joined defence academy, and deserted. In a few months I hoped to find my

professional bearing though I knew not what at present...'(COK 121)

Here dream, dialogue, and song are employed to depict changing attitudes in the consciousness of the young hero. In six years of transition Yoyo had run his wit's end at various jobs –including fatherhood– and here he is a reluctant returnee. Earlier determined on a course of total self-exile, he had never wanted to set foot on his home town any more but the strong pull to be present at grand dad's funeral reveals a quality of loyalty and citizenship in the young hero.

Yoyo's dream entries had presaged the passage of the old grandparents signifying a passage of a generation. Dream recording is significant of a rising awareness of himself and the dialogue in this section is no longer lengthy for young Yoyo had other thoughts to occupy him.

> Ham drove roughly and jerkily. 'I am just coming from your compound, your old Bap's wake keeping is tonight,' he told me sanguinely.
> 'Is that so?' I now knew where he had had his drink.
> 'Oh, you didn't know this?' he remarked, a little surprised at my ignorance. I explained.' I got Mam's letter and I thought so.'
> 'That's tomorrow. Tonight is the keeping awake for all night,' and he proceeded to chatter through the rest of the journey but my attention was somewhere else. (COK 134)

Goodman has also changed. He now wears 'a distant contemplative expression on his face' in fulfilment of Old Bap's injunction for him to go into 'studied contemplation' for the rest of his life. Bap shows 'a tacit note of comprehension' towards Yoyo. The circumstance of the changing awareness may be old Bap's transition. Yoyo was not present at the

19

funeral of Kata and Big Mam. Now Old Bap's which he witnesses is rendered in poetic sympathy: 'Thus draped in this still silent depth of profundity, my grand dad slept. (135)'

The songs of the preceding events have paled in comparison with the funeral songs; they now carry a sombre reverence as against the comic irreverence of the earlier ones, probably due to the occasion of death. But unlike the prodigal son, Yoyo's return is not permanent. Yoyo is leaving town the next day after the burial. The suggestion of continuity is made poignant in the dialogue with the old breed who angle for a second burial suggesting attachment to the old values and ways of life. Yoyo tells Mabelle:

> The burial is over now, ...I mean Old Bap is buried, and that's more important (than a merely ceremonial and economically wasteful second burial) (146)

Yoyo is thinking he should be getting back to (his) own life and more especially back to (his) child and her mother....(146). A new attitude of introspective cognition (thought/memory) rather than the interactive sessions (dialogue) emerges from the discourse of the old breed and two young members of the new generation, being Yoyo and Dora. Dora avoids everyone's eyes with 'placid disinterest.' The narrator remarks that her capacity to retain her opinions to herself, which surpassed that of the Virgin Mary, had given him a clue as to the new attitude of goodwill he must show his people. It is not the critical, deprecatory attitude of past story narratives. It is the goodwill from a mutual parting of ways made smoother by the deeper level of understanding that had been foreshadowed in *An African Eclipse*.

> I have chosen now the day is bright
> (the shining light of

soul lights) the middle lonely route.(AE 3)

For young Yoyo it is a lonely route to an era devoted an understanding an acceptance of the onus of self-responsibility.

Time, Memory and Illusion in *The Visitor*

The Visitor, described as Chin Ce's full length novel and third in his published series, takes an entirely new approach to modern story telling in Africa. It is a story in which three dimensions of existence affecting three principal players Erie, Mensa, and Deego interrelate continuously to create an unbreakable thread and posit a statement on the continuation of individual responsibility over and above mere existential needs. The philosophy behind the whole story seems to be predicated upon an Igbo traditional song a translation of the main part which appears before the story:

> We are visitors upon this earth
> This world is not our own
> We have come but to a market place
> Only to purchase and go home

It would be therefore correct to state that the story teller is here concerned with the individual's quest for wholeness (the search for purpose) signified in Erie's lost memory (TV 1). For the hero, the discovery of who he is, and what he was, spans three paradigms of awareness –the past, present and future earlier mentioned. Erie, Mensa, and Deego are therefore same individuals as are Zeta, Sena, and Sarah in the deliberate tripartite also signified in the three suns of Erin ancestral land.

The setting in the future (2040) comes to us in the end part of the story as an epilogue and we are surprised to realise the whole story may have been cut from a movie which the viewer Deego had watched the night before he dozes off into an entirely strange adventure of a past dimension of reality. The movie scenes apparently trigger some series of experiences which draw back to a past history of crime and death featuring Mensa in 1994. In this city called Aja, a cult mentality permeates the society and the youths have lost their sense of values.

Yet this past is integrated within another world (Erin land) of an advanced line of kinsmen who live up to their roles as healers and teachers of the race. Mensa now called Erie in the land of his ancestors must go back and retrieve his memory lost from the gun blast that took his life on earth.

Mensa is the product of the herd syndrome and violence that riddle the nation and threaten to destroy its entire fabric of existence. Unlike Yoyo, he never graduates from college. His drop out of school is the natural consequence of his denial of creative and positive existence, and added with his misguided involvement in the quest of revenge, Mensa's destruction appears a foregone conclusion.

The 1994 story of Mensa is seen partly through his narrative consciousness and through the omniscient narrative point of view to embrace a world of police corruption and decadence in Nigeria, a country drowning in its own degenerate materialism. All it offers may just be frustration and disappointment at all levels, a frustration that permeates Mensa's efforts and dogs all his noxious attempts at identity through cult power.

Ironi alone of all the others enjoyed tacit state patronage and confidence. It warmed his heart to know then that the minister of

22

petroleum was one of the financiers of the club. Thus even as a job seeker Ironi connection guaranteed a niche among the notables of the society in which he had sought social acceptance, if only he could work hard enough in service to earn his cut and launch himself into wealth and power!

How could it have been otherwise? Better put, why did it become otherwise now? (TV 40)

In contrast to this world is Erin, the land of the ancestors as a present reality. The author's entry into the subjective universe of ancestral interactivity offers a unique perspective on contemporaneous and simultaneous levels of existence. Surprisingly in this world of the ancestors is a highly advanced city where even the memory of the individual members of the race can be retrieved and preserved for healing purposes or for posterity. The ancestral universe is thus not unlike the parallel worlds of modern science fiction where the author must have drawn his influence. But the idyllic representation of this world of ancestors as custodian of the African heritage is a product of a conscious artiste who wishes to consolidate the belief in the race through the emergence of a progeny who will eventually take charge of the transcendent responsibilities of heritage.

Thus Mensa now as Erin is seen living another existence in Erin City –a temporary existence that offers recovery from the modernist adventurism of his physical life.

It plagued him daily to walk about the walls of the city like some disembodied entity, a ghost whose only memory of his identity comes in flashes and hunches.

'You are at home among your spirits,' Zeta's granddad told him. 'But you will not understand, and it were better you did not ask too much questions. Take those daydreams, visions and nightmares as natural as the colour of your tan, things which will continue to hold

23

little value to you until you come to face your past in order to know the moment (22)

This spiritual universe comes in grasps or strains of recollection where time is of a different scale and values are quite unlike those of the material plane. Thus the process of healing may take some time not only for Erie but for the whole society afflicted by the plague of displacement and lack of sympathy.

> The city of his fathers looked all strange to him. Broad cleanly swept roads and walkways. All so real too. But then reality he had now learnt was a relative thing. He couldn't believe he had lived here for seven years, seven good years that seemed like seven hundred years in earth's span and still no concrete or tangible evidence of who he truly was (22)

Finally the time comes, almost too soon, for Erie to withdraw from this idealised world of communal empathy to face the full details of his actions as Mensa on the physical terrain. The rest of the story moves quickly leading to the summation of characters in the story and their relationship with one another.

Important characters in this part include Sena and Omo, both allies of Mensa in the robbery and search for vengeance. The deaths of the characters come in swift ironic successions both allies dying by the hand of their friend Mensa, and Mensa finally falling to summary execution by armed militia men by which the Nigerian society, where the setting is derived, is sorely notorious for. In the replay of the death experience, Mensa's memory is transferred to Erie who now metamorphoses in Erin City with a wider perspective of his part in the rhythm of life. Erie discovers that Zeta (Sena) has been there all the time and both of them must continue the quest for further understanding of themselves and their lives' purpose.

The Visitor is a blend of the subjective consciousness in a serious quest for identity. True to opinion (TV1), it will remain a serious challenge to the traditional view of time and reality as a linear or progressive sequence of events. This is a major attribute of the new oeuvres. This approach to fiction in Africa may appear to hold some significance beyond the ordinary and subjective perspective of social reality. In comparison to Lawrence's idea of art assisting in the living of life to the fullest (*Sons* xvii), the cyclic universe of memory, transition and dialogue undoubtedly presents a far deeper conception of art, and of life, that centres on the individual's perception of his unique position in society.

Chapter Two

The Two Tragedies

K. Usongo

Introduction

WE must stress the link between superstition and morality in the plays of William Shakespeare and the novels of Chinua Achebe. It is argued that even though over 400 years separate both writers, the theme of superstition is taken up by both artists and they view it as a moral antenna to their respective societies.

Achebe, in his writings, depicts superstition as deeply rooted among the Ibo. The fate of his central characters, namely, Okonkwo, Ezeulu, and Obi Okonkwo appear to be remotely guided by external forces. And these outside forces constantly step in the action to sanction vice and to reward virtue. This leaves one with the feeling that external forces and man seem to be inextricably woven. Shakespeare, on the other hand, portrays an Elizabethan society that is at crossroads of the supernatural. The Elizabethans apparently manifest congenital traits of superstition as some of them battle with it. Macbeth, Othello, and Brutus are typical examples. Whether accepted as the mainstream of their lives or rejected outright, superstition is shown as the common denominator between these two writers as they portray the viewpoints of their respective societies to it: the one relishing it gingerly, the other overtly embracing it. In other words, myriads of

26

nameless spirits are believed to besiege the earth and man's life is caught up with the activities of these dynamic and ferocious forces.

D. H. Lawrence believed that the purpose of art was not simply to give enjoyment. He asserted that he wrote because he wanted English folk to alter, and to have more sense. Considering the challenges posed by Shakespearean and Achebean tragedies in terms of the very engaging subjects handled, there is grave doubt that a reader of them will remain unperturbed. The politically orchestrated murders, the villainies perpetuated by vicious characters and the consequences of their actions on themselves, the community and the state will, doubtlessly, leave the spectators and readers enlightened. Indeed, the final words of Harolde sum up the principle of the gods rewarding good and sanctioning vice:

> Let no man thinke by fetches finely filde, by double driftes convayed cunningly, to get or gayne by any craft or guile, A good estate with long prosperitie. His lust obtaynde, he lives in miserie, his guilty ghost dooth see his plague appeare, Who goeth straight he needeth not to feare (Campbell 9).

Superstition as an unreasoning awe or fear of something unknown, mysterious, or imaginary, especially in connection with religion; religious belief or practice founded upon fear or ignorance. In this same dictionary, magic is defined as the pretended art of influencing the course of events, and of producing marvellous physical phenomena by processes supposed to owe their efficacy to their power of compelling the intervention of spiritual beings or of bringing into operation some controlling principle of nature such as sorcery or witchcraft. In its widest sense, superstition seems to be an inherent part of the human mind - what Hugh Miller named "the workings of that religion natural to the human heart." Morality can be seen as poetic justice which is a convention in literature whereby virtue is compensated and evil punished either by man or supernatural agents. In *King Lear*, it is seemingly absent in the main plot, but features in the subplot.₁ Having failed to be flattered by Cordelia, Lear, in a fit of passion, solemnly swears by some deities for a rupture in his relationship with her:

> by the sacred radiance of the sun,
> The mysteries of Hecate, and the night; By all the operations of the orbs
> From whom we do exist and cease to be;
> Here I disclaim all my paternal care;(1.i:105-109)

These mysterious sources of nature that Lear refers to reflect his violent passion against Cordelia. The sun god, Apollo, and night goddess, Hecate, that he invokes were deities worshipped by ancient priests of Britain, Gaul and Ireland. This appeal to these gods represents the elemental impulse of superstition in Lear.

Kent intervenes on behalf of Cordelia, pleading with Lear to revoke his curses on her. He argues that he cannot be indifferent to the folly and madness of the king in thinking that Cordelia loves him least. Lear is angry, and swears by Apollo to harm Kent. He banishes him from Britain and affirms this in the name of Jupiter, the God that controls the affairs of men. When Goneril humiliates Lear by proposing to reduce his retinue, he regrets having misjudged Cordelia, and prays to the nature goddess to render Goneril sterile:

Hear, nature, hear; dear goddess, hear! Suspend thy purposes; if thou didst intend To make this creature fruitful!
Into her womb convey sterility!
Dry up in her the organs of increase,
And from her derogate body never spring A babe to honour her! If she must teem, Create her child of spleen, that it may live And be a thwart, disnatured torment to her! (1.iv:260-269)

Knowing that it is difficult for him to punish Goneril for disrespect, he resorts to nature which here is a custodian of justice. Albany is baffled at such display of cruelty by Goneril: "Now, gods that we adore, whereof comes this?" (1.iv:275). Lear's mind is tempestuous and he verges on the point of madness; he appears to be under forces other than himself: "O, let me not be mad, not mad, sweet heaven! / keep me in temper; I would not be mad" (1.v:38-39).

When Cornwall challenges Kent on the question of his moral uprightness, the latter defends his impeccable reputation by swearing by Phoebus that is also seen as a harbinger of adversity.

When Lear is further incensed by Regan's refusal to accommodate his attendants, he sees in the raging storm an attempt by the gods to torment evil doers:

Let the great gods,
That keep this dreadful pudder o'er our heads, Find out their enemies now.
(111.ii:48-49).

On his part, Gloucester attributes human suffering to the gods, and argues that human destiny is at the mercy of the gods whom he urges to institute justice on transgressors:

29

Let the superfluous and lust-dieted man, That slaves your ordinance, that will not see Because he does not feel, feel your power quickly;
So distribution should undo excess
And each man have enough. (IV.ii:67-71)

In the same vein, Albany solicits the heavens to punish Goneril for tormenting Lear and Gloucester. As if the gods were listening to his appeal, a messenger reports on the death of Cornwall; Albany is vindicated when he remarks:

This shows you are above
You justicers, that these our nether crimes
So proudly can venge. (IV.ii: 78-80)

Kent echoes Albany when he emphasizes, concerning fate, that "It is the stars, / The stars above us, govern our conditions" (IV.iii: 32-33).

When Edgar slays Edmund in a duel, the former underscores the crucial role of the gods: "They are just, and of our pleasant vices /make instruments to plague us" (V. iii: 170). Therefore Gloucester's extramarital relationship cost him the loss of sight, and Edmund's vaulting ambition death. Samuel Johnson says in relation to King Lear that Shakespeare's enabling of Edmund to co-operate with the chief design whereby perfidy is combined with perfidy, a wicked son aligns with wicked daughters, is to present the moral that villainy is never at a stop, that crimes lead to crimes, and at last terminate in ruin (Bratchell 121)

Macbeth is plagued by a vision of Banquo's ghost which none but him sees. We learn that the return of this ghost, like so many similar apparitions in Elizabethan and Jacobean drama, is a visual reminder of unrevenged crimes and imminent retribution (Mehl 121-122). Macbeth naively counts on the witches' prophecy that declares his invincibility. He is slain in a fight with Macduff who had earlier sworn to quieten the ghosts of his wife and children that Macbeth slew. Lady Macbeth's sleep-walking pushes her to disclose her hideous contribution in the death of Duncan. She is fond of rubbing her hands in an attempt to redeem her blighted conscience. Frustration preys on her and she is driven into committing suicide.

The defeat of the conspirators in Julius Caesar is largely the result of retribution. Brutus attributes their misfortune in the war against Mark Antony to the making of Caesar:

> O Julius Caesar, thou art mighty yet, Thy spirit walks abroad, and turns ourSwords
> In air against our proper entrails (V.iii:94-96)

He begs his servant to murder him because Caesar's ghost appeared before him three times; to him, this means that "my hour is come" (V.v:19). John Arthos rightly makes a comparison between the witches in Macbeth and the ghosts in Julius Caesar that these features bring with them clear notions of fate and destiny and justice (Arthos 158)

The appearance of the ghost before Hamlet suggests some foul play within the kingdom; its visitation jostles young Hamlet from lethargy by convincing him that his suspicions on Claudius are justified. Claudius' death can be seen as the work of the ghost since its mission of revenge is apparently achieved though some people might argue that Claudius' death is accidental with Hamlet not avenging as his father ordered. A.C. Bradley posits that the ghost is the representative of that hidden ultimate power, the messenger of divine justice set upon the expiation of offences which appeared impossible for man to discover and avenge (Bradley 141).

In the Achebean novels, the gods act as moral authorities within the society as is true of Ani that ensures good conduct and morality by rejecting suicide. As a result, if a man kills himself, he is not buried by his kinsmen because he has desecrated the land. In *Arrow of God*, Umuaro's defeat in the war with Okperi is ascribed to the former's neglect of Ulu's instruction. In declaring war on Okperi, Umuaro had challenged the deity which laid the foundation of their village. The disputed piece of land rightfully belongs to Okperi as seen in the fact that the gods side with the real owners of the land. Okoye's death, coming on the heels of his brother's, is attributed to Ekwensu.

The sacred python belongs to Idemili and it is understood that no harm should be done to it. Any threat to its life risks calamity for the entire clan. Even the christian Moses Unachukwu's account of the creation of Umuaro attests this. The story goes that six brothers of Umuama killed the python, prepared yam pottage with it and shared among themselves. Quarreling and fighting soon cropped up among the brothers and stretched across Umuama. Many lost their lives and the surrounding villages were scared, and consulted a deity. They were told never to kill the sacred python. It is this python that Oduche imprisons; his action demands serious cleansing. His mother, Ugoye, looks forward to the Festival of the Pumpkin Leaves with anxiety; it would afford her an opportunity to avert any disaster provoked by her son's defilement of the land. As Ezeulu paces on the ceremonial ground, women wave leaves round their heads and throw on the fleeing chief priest. This symbolizes a fervent appeal to Ulu to cleanse Umuaro of any impurities. Ugoye's prayer buttresses this point:

Great Ulu who kills and saves, I implore you to cleanse my household of all defilement. If I have spoken it with my mouth or seen it with my eyes, or if I have heard it with my ears or stepped on it with my foot or if it has come through my children or my friends or kinsfolk let it follow these leaves (*Arrow* 72).

Ezeulu's contemplation of revenge on Umuaro for abandoning him in the crisis with the white man is dissuaded by Ulu. However, the stubborn priest is determined to retaliate during the feast of the New Yam. He refuses to listen to the pleas of the elders that he eats the remaining yams and convene the feast. He feigns sympathy for the ordinary Umuaro man and states that the gods at times use them as a whip. He argues that Ulu is unhappy because no one broke kolanut for him for the past two months. Starvation creeps into the land and many people dissociate themselves from the chief priest.

He is increasingly isolated since some people hold that he is seeking personal revenge on Umuaro. Many join the ranks of Christians in search of protection against the wrath of Ulu. The consequence of Ezeulu's behaviour is swift and drastic. He becomes demented and Obika's death, to Ezidemili, "should teach him (Ezeulu) how far he could dare next time" (228).

The influence of the gods is also felt in the Oso Nwanadi, a retreat organized by the six villages to appease the angry spirits of kinsmen killed in war or made to suffer death in the interest of Umuaro. In Umuachala, the Akwu Nro, a ritual involving prayers and offerings by widows for departed husbands, is celebrated. On the eve of this ritual, every widow prepares foofoo and palm nut soup and places outside the hut. The widows wake up in the morning and find the bowls empty, the contents having been eaten by their late husbands residing in Ani-Mmo. At times, a mask is presented during one of such rituals and no woman is expected to disclose the identity of the person wearing it. If she disobeys this injunction, she may be rendered sterile, mad or even dead.

Behind the Okwolo, a house in which people initiated into the mystery of ancestral spirits watch displays, is found the sacred udala tree. No one is supposed to harvest any fruit from it. If he violates this rule, he would be visited by all the Masked spirits in Umuaro and "he would have to wipe off their footsteps with heavy fines and sacrifices" (196).

In *Things Fall Apart*, Okonkwo is punished by Ezeani, priest of the earth goddess, for violating the week of peace. This week is considered sacred and the entire clan is expected to radiate joy, kindness, warmth and peace. Okonkwo is provoked by the negligence of Ojiugo, his third wife, who instead of preparing a meal for her husband, goes to plait her hair. This earns her a beating from him. In the face of this abomination, disaster can be averted only when Okonkwo heeds the priest's instruction of bringing to the shrine of Ani a she-goat, a hen, a length of cloth and a hundred cowries.

The Egwugwu is the most powerful cult in Iboland. It acts as an agent of justice, listening to complaints and proposing solutions. It is thanks to it that Uzowulu's marriage is repaired when it states that his in-laws should drink his wine and return his wife.

It is unimaginable that a man can unmask an egwugwu in public or blaspheme its unblemished reputation. The overzealous christian, Enoch, stretches his hand too far by exposing this spirit to the full glare of women and children, an act that sows confusion in Umuofia. Because of this abomination, the Mother Spirit is restless, walking throughout the night and mourning for her murdered son. We are told that:

> it was a terrible night. Not even the oldest man in Umuofia had ever heard such a strange and fearful sound ... It seemed as if the very soul of the tribe wept for a great evil that was coming-its own death (132)..

The fiery band of spirits heads for Enoch's compound. Even the white priest, Smith, is cowed. In a split second, Enoch's compound is reduced to rubble, and the church to ashes.

Okonkwo's killing of Ezeudu's son is considered a female crime in Umuofia. It is involuntary and merits seven years of exile. Men of Umuofia, dressed in battle gear, demolish his compound and ravage his barns. This destruction is seen as a fulfillment of the justice of the earth goddess that acts vicariously through these men. After all, Okonkwo had earlier offended her by killing Ikemefuna. Obierika, at one time, was forced to swallow the will of the earth goddess when she decreed that his wife's twin children be destroyed because they were an offence to the land. Okoli's death is attributed to his killing of the royal python.

Shakespeare and Achebe are concerned with issues of morality as their works are couched in societies under the grip of superstition. Shakespeare uses this medium to strengthen virtue through an inducement of honourable actions and ideas. He is a writer of immense intellect. His art form involves the vivid stage impersonation of human beings challenging sympathy and commanding varied participation. In his plays, a wide range of characters are opposed or contrasted; and the action displays their antagonisms and attractions, provoking a gamut of reactions.

For his world is one in which men and women reveal their minds, sustain our sympathy or disgust and hold our anxiety at what innocent and subtle minds are able to do.

A reading of the tragedies of Shakespeare and the novels of Achebe shows comparative indices between Achebe and Shakespeare, especially in the coincidences noted in certain situations. There is a strong indication that the African novelist was particularly moved by Shakespeare's Macbeth. The following illustrations attest this. Okonkwo's outrageous killing of Ikemefuna calls to mind Macbeth's atrocious murder of Banquo.

Okonkwo's restlessness results from this callous murder in the same way as Macbeth is plunged into a crisis of insecurity and anguish because of his killing of innocent Duncan. The child's spirit harasses Okonkwo, reducing him to a puny thing just as Banquo's ghost haunts Macbeth. Okonkwo and Macbeth are conceived as great soldiers who, at critical moments, cannot overcome their fear. Initially, both command respect within their respective communities, but they die ignoble deaths.

Ezeulu's visit to the Oracle of the Caves and Hills to inquire whether to convene the yam festival or not reminds us of Macbeth's visit to the witches to know about his future. Ezeulu says that the oracles are against celebrating the festival; an interpretation that is disputable just as the witches' metaphorical explanation to Macbeth that he can only be destroyed when Birnam wood moves to Dunsinane and that none of woman born can harm him. Obika's death signals doom for Ezeulu in the same way as Lady Macbeth's to Macbeth; these two can be seen as the alter egoes of the heroes. They lose their pillars of support, and are now saddled by events. Dieter Mehl aptly comments in relation to Macbeth, Claudius, Iago and Edmund that their well- deserved exposure

36

is not a central aspect of the tragic impact, but the confirmation of moral order and poetic justice (105.

In Shakespearean drama, the voice of morality appears muffled and comes to life more through supernatural forces in the forms of ghosts and ancient gods and goddesses such as Apollo, Janus and Hecate. The whole action of his tragedy is enveloped in the mystery of unleashed actions that constantly surprise us. Beyond these happenings hovers the shadow of the supernatural. Local deities are assigned guardianship over specific local life interests and concerns. Myriads of nameless spirits are thought to besiege the earth and man's life is caught up with the activities of these dynamic and ferocious forces. The network of sacred figures, images, beliefs and ideas which form the traditional vision of the cosmos help Achebean characters in the compelling quest of being able to explain, predict and control events. (Ejizu 118-120)

In Achebe's novels, morality is overtly stated in the actions of gods through their custodians that bring to order erring people or inflict harm on them to deter others. This is probably the role of Ala, the earth goddess, that acts as a moralizing force in society through her guidance of her laws and punishment of offenders. The case of Okonkwo who is singled out for disgrace and destruction by her is illustrative. Men recognize the fact that the gods have a will of their own and cannot be merely manipulated by men, who must be submissive and humble before them.(Turner 8)

In fact, the element of superstition adds artistic complexity to the tragedies of Shakespeare and Achebe; it gives their art density and scope and makes it look beyond the modalities of time and place. Above all, this theme, through its integration of morality, enhances the readability of Shakespeare and Achebe.

Chapter Three

New Male Characters

M.C.Gyimah

IN *The Art of Ama Ata Aidoo: Polylectics and Reading Against Neo- colonialism,* Vincent Odamtten argues that Aidoo's works consistently address the issue of neo-colonialism and its impact on the educated Ghanaian elite. Citing critics like Omolara Ogundipe-Leslie who maintains that the African woman writer has a particular commitment to discuss issues of gender, womanhood and a Third World reality, and Ngugi wa Thiong'o who asserts that African writers must write against neo-colonialism, Odamtten stresses that readers and critics of African literature should also invest in reading and writing against neo-colonialism. He says, "[i]f there are writers who are writing against neo-colonialism, there should be reader-critics who complement their work" (6). He warns against reading and writing about African women characters and situations from a narrow feminist perspective. Such criticism which sometimes focuses on the ills of patriarchy through colonial impositions and those effected through "indigenous pre-colonial values and relations" promote a dichotomous analysis of African literature (4). Odamtten, then, argues for a polylectic approach to reading and critiquing these works. He says that in order to read in this manner, one must "begin to develop a polylectic understanding of Africa's economic, political, and cultural actualities" (6). Hence, a polylectic criticism will require that a work of art be approached in a

> self-interpellative manner, bringing to our reading and critique enough knowledge that our evaluation may account for as many of the complexities of the specific (con)text of the literary/cultural product as possible...A polylectic criticism acknowledges the *interdependencies* even as it recognizes the over determinate autonomies of the writer, text, audience and social whole. (5)

In reading/ writing against (neo)colonialism, a careful consideration of the experience of occupied nations must be made. While we may be aware of such issues as political dominance, language and religious appropriation, it is also important to look more closely at the forced conditions and influences that impacted the African and, in this case, the African male. It is often at this level that African writers involve their characters and works. If we are to complement African writers' works as reader-critics of (neo)colonialism, we should be able to understand this condition. As Aidoo puts it, we have to be able to think about this issue and understand the most frightening experience of colonialism, the effect it has had on our minds (Odamtten 17).

Scholars such as Frantz Fanon, Aime Cesaire, and W. E. B Du Bois have discussed the effects of colonialism and particularly the psychological harm that caused to the colonised. Their critical works uncompromisingly expose the colonial enterprise, clearly defining the coloniser's position as master, the subjugation of colonised people, and the consequences of the entire experience onoppressed. In the *Discourse on Colonialism*, Aime Cesaire defines colonialism as a tool of oppression and a destruction of humanity which was enacted under the guise of a civilizing mission (11-

12). Cesaire explains that colonialism was motivated by white supremacist convictions to historicise Africans, subordinate them and claim their resources. Claiming their bodies as objects and discarding their world view(s) as primitive and inferior, colonialism, then, was a source of devastation to their very foundation and lives. Fanon makes similar arguments in *Black Skin White Masks* and charges that the enforcement of European ideals and a supposed superior way of life on the victim destroys his value of self and culture and therefore prompts him to run away from his African identity and to annihilate his own presence (*Black Skin* 60). This condition is what Ngugi wa Thiong'o has referred to as "the cultural bomb." Ngugi puts forth that the cultural bomb is the biggest weapon wielded and unleashed by colonialism. Responding to the cultural bomb by running away from his individuality, the colonised embraces Western ideals; furthermore, wanting to identify with the master, he eventually desires to abandon his post and undertake the role of the coloniser himself.

According to Fanon,

> the look that the native turns on the settler's town is a look of envy; it expresses his dreams of possession -all manner of possession: to sit at the settler's table, to sleep in the settler's bed, with his wife if possible. The colonised man is an envious man...It is true, for there is no native who does not dream at least once a day of setting himself up in the settler's place. (*The Wretched* 39)

Fanon's argument explains the behaviours of colonised persons- turned oppressors. The historical account of Americo-Liberians attests to this as well as the behaviours of many Western educated Africans who return to their countries and assume a superior attitude towards other natives. Furthermore, African writers like Aidoo express this sentiment in their writing. However, one tends to differ with Fanon that it is inevitable that all natives dream of assuming the settler's place as this is disproved by the liberatory efforts of African people. Aidoo's short story "For Whom Things Did Not Change," illustrates where the cook for a member of the elite admits his surprise that his new master does not act like the others.

Fanon's theory of an identity crisis is also elaborated by Du Bois in *The Souls of Black Folk*. Although Du Bois is referring to the African American experience as regarding white racism, it is applicable to other colonised subjects because of the common encounter with the Western world. Du Bois explains that because of slavery and racist politics in the United States, the African American finds he has a dual identity which he must grapple with daily. "The Negro," he explains,

> is a sort of seventh son, born with a veil, and gifted with second sight in this American world, -a world which yields him no true self-consciousness, but only lets him see himself through the revelation of the other world. It is a peculiar sensation, this double-consciousness, this sense of always looking at one's self through the eyes of others, of measuring one's soul by the tape of a world that looks on in amused contempt and pity. One ever feels his twoness, - an American, a Negro; two souls, two thoughts, two unreconciled strivings; two warring ideals in one dark body, whose dogged strength alone keeps it from being torn asunder. (45)

Thus the Negro is trapped between looking at and presenting himself from two irresolvable perceptions as a result of a racist- colonial history. Hence, with Du Bois' double consciousness, there seem to be an inability to come to a specific claim of self. However, the concept of double consciousness may have been challenged by Jamaica Kincaid's account on the dilemma of a colonial influenced identity.

41

While Kincaid will acknowledge the validity of this condition, she will argue that one can reconcile his identity by stepping out of the confines that dictate and impose certain ideals and definitions on the self. She illustrates this in her short essay "On Seeing England for the First Time" and her novels, particularly, *Annie John* and *Lucy*. Kincaid presents the damaging effects caused by the colonial mandate of discarding one's native culture and replacing it with a more "legitimate" one.

However, Aidoo goes further in her critique of neo-colonialism. Through her works, she demonstrates that a reading against (neo)colonialism must acknowledge the connectedness of different forms of oppression (Odamtten 125). In so doing, she provides a challenging and complex view of issues with which the reader

/audience is to grapple. Her discussion does not simply end at the level of the forced master /slave relationship between the European and the African but continues with an exploration of other oppressive and exploitative situations resulting from that experience. What Aidoo in fact does is to illustrate, to a certain extent, the validity of Fanon's theory and take it a little further. As Carole Boyce Davies would put it, she goes a piece of the way with it (*Black Women's Writing*). Regarding the neo-colonial discussion, she presents that the double conscious male that Du Bois discusses does not always remain in a subordinate position but can choose to draw a conscious line (Kincaid) thereby separating himself from his fellow victims. While this separation does not necessarily erase his relationship to the coloniser, it however provides for him a continuation or perhaps a recreation of the very relationship he was once subjected to, hence, Fanon's victim turned victimiser.

Aidoo connects colonialism to sexism by arguing that part of the effects of (neo)colonialism is sexism. Making the connection between the two oppressions isn't to imply that she necessarily parallels the two as equal and simultaneous, neither is it an argument that it is a matter of cause and effect as if to say that sexism is strictly a result of European influence. What she however presents is that while gender oppression was relevant in pre-colonial Africa, colonial influence led to a greater form of sexism.

In an interview with Adeola James, she says,

[i]t is quite ridiculous, really, that people, especially educated African men, operate as though women were not around. That is part of the colonial inheritance, because it wasn't like that in our societies, at least not in most of them. Although, at every stage, women have not been given that headship position, our societies have not been totally oblivious of the presence and existence of women. I think it is part of that whole colonial rubbish that our men behave the way they do. (24)

Aidoo is not the only one to make this argument. In her work *Male Daughters, Female Husbands*, Ifi Amadiume maintains that colonialism "eroded" the African woman's traditional access to social and political power and influence. The imposed colonial separation between men and women in respect to power and privilege exacerbated any pre- existing gender inequalities. She says that in pre-colonial Africa, a flexible gender system, which allowed male roles opened to certain categories of women, placed women in a more favourable position for the acquisition of wealth and formal political power and authority (123). However, "under colonialism, these indigenous institutions - condemned by the churches as '"pagan'" and anti-Christian- were abandoned or reinterpreted to the detriment of women" (123).

While colonial legislation effected change on traditional African women's lives as maintained by the above arguments, Aidoo further illustrates in her works that it is not only the enforcement of Euro- Christian doctrines that engendered these aberrations. Rather as the slave yearns for his master's status, he begins to imitate and enforce his oppressor's actions. Because his maleness is privileged, he could then be justified to assert power over the woman. He discovers that empowerment is granted through the act of exploitation. In *Our Sister Killjoy,* Sissie, the critical eye and voice against (neo)colonial, imperial and sexist oppression finds herself savouring, although momentarily, the empowerment that domination rewards. By recreating a heterosexual dynamic in a possible lesbian relationship between Sissie and Marija, Aidoo shows that altering the players can sometimes be simply a repetition of what is an established and familiar practice. Confronted with a physical and emotional lesbian proposal, Sissie imagines and wishes she were a man (67). And as the relationship further takes the structure of a heterosexual power play with Marija expressing the views of the unappreciated and emotionally abused woman, Sissie does become the man.

[s]uddenly, something exploded in Sissie like fire. She did not know exactly what it was. It was not painful. It did not hurt. On the contrary, it was a pleasurable heat. Because as she watched the other woman standing there, now biting her lips, now gripping at the handle of her baby's pram and looking so generally disorganised, she, Sissie wanted to laugh and laugh and laugh. Clearly, she was enjoying herself to see that woman hurt. It was nothing she had desired, Nor did it seem as if she could control it, this inhuman sweet sensation to see another human being squirming. It hit her like a stone, the knowledge that there is pleasure in hurting. A strong three-dimensional pleasure, an

exclusive masculine delight that is exhilarating beyond all measure.
And this too is God's gift to man? She wondered. (75-76)

Aidoo makes it clear that "Sissie felt like a bastard. Not a bitch. A bastard" (75). This can be read as a reversal of the coloniser and colonised. The politically radical Sissie easily trades places with Marija, the European woman, her (once) oppressor and begins to enjoy her ability to exert some form of authority over her. This is not to suggest that Sissie suffers from double consciousness because it is clear throughout *Killjoy* what her position is. But with this instance, Aidoo notes that even those most certain about identity and critical on matters of oppression can become vulnerable to this "masculine delight that is exhilarating beyond all measure" (76). Thus, with a mention of this "masculine delight" and "God's gift to man," which resound the argument of manifest destiny and the White man's burden, Aidoo again connects colonial privilege to masculine authority.

In his analysis of *Anowa*, Lloyd Brown notes this link made by Aidoo and posits that because of her presentation of some female characters' endorsement of the status quo, such as the old woman of "The Mouth That Eats Salt and Pepper," Aidoo abstains from portraying the problem as an exclusively male one. He continues that "although the distinguishing norms of male behaviour are stamped with a male preoccupation with power, the real issue is that power has become a corrupting and destructive force in both cultures simply because the power-brokers, who happen to be male, have been corrupted by the basis and nature of their power rather than by their male identity" (Brown 94). Brown's point is supported by Aidoo when she makes it clear in her interview with Adeola James that she does not believe in sexual warfare and that her works are not meant to be read as such. Hence

45

Aidoo confirms that although the different oppressions are connected, it is rather the claim for power that initiates conflict. The desire to feel empowered leads Sissie to abuse Marija emotionally. But Sissie decides to withdraw from such abuse when "she became aware of the fact that she would do something quite crazy if she continued on that trail of mind" (76). Nevertheless, we find that quite a few of "our men," as Aidoo would put it, do not engage in a consciousness that suggests abstinence from an abusive position. Rather, desiring to escape their reduced status, to acquire that of the master and to further sense this empowerment and "exclusive masculine delight," certain men do not only claim the authority of the master but, by asserting their maleness, also colonise the body of their women.

Within the three works, *The Dilemma of a Ghost*, *Anowa*, and *Changes*, Aidoo portrays male characters of the African elite who are undoubtedly subjects of (neo)colonialism. While two of these men, Ato Yawson and Ali Kondey are products of (neo)colonialism and Western education, Kofi Ako is however not formally educated and is situated in the colonial period of Ghana, the then Gold Coast. Despite the different eras, Aidoo nonetheless demonstrates the crises that the European influence has caused in the lives of these different men. It is this influence that shapes their characters and their relationships with women.

In her first play, *The Dilemma of a Ghost,* Aidoo presents a Ghanaian neo-colonial elite who cannot reconcile his double consciousness. Odamtten explains that to use the dilemma tale in order to bring light to Ato Yawson's situation is telling in itself because "essentially, the dilemma tale is a narrative whose primary function is to stimulate serious, deep-probing discussions of social, political, and moral issues that confront human beings in their everyday lives" (18). Formally educated in America, Ato Yawson returns home with his African American wife Eulalie. Western education has effected change in Ato. He fails to meet cultural expectations and avoids taking responsibilities for the consequences. Ato represents the confused and lost "been-to." Odamtten says,

> the been-to is usually characterized as suffering the double estrangement of the sujet -en soi: [one who is caught between two conflicting ideological practices] rejected by or rejecting his or her "African culture" by virtue of higher education on the one hand, and simultaneously rejected by or rejecting Western bourgeois culture by virtue of his or her colour. The been-to is thus a paradox who, for the "loved ones," augurs the possibility of surmounting the restrictions and limitations of their neo-colonial reality. (31)

The obvious ideological oppositions of the African and Western backgrounds hinder Ato's determination of an identity. The dilemma is whether he is able to abandon the foreign ideals he encountered and to continue as expected in his country. By closely looking at Ato and the actions he takes, a second but related concern becomes whether he is willing to separate himself from the West. As his dream and the dilemma song reveal, he is caught at a crossroads and is confused about what he should do.

Aidoo opens the play and immediately informs the audience about the situation at hand. The narrator makes it known that a son of the clan is returning from "the white man's land" (2) and that there are certain expectations required of him. The narrator relates that while Ato will work in the city, he is expected to return home now and then on weekends and on festive occasions. And also that as a child of the country and the clan, it is only natural that he comes home for blessings when the new yam has been harvested and the Stools are sprinkled (2). Note that the narrator casually relates this information as if to say that this is obviously taken for granted. But within the narration, Aidoo has already established the conflict as the narrator speaks of a "scholar" performing traditional rites. The narrator and the community fail to realize that trained in the Western atmosphere which espouses Eurocentrism, Ato, like the common been-to will not easily fall back into his communal role. By already drawing the two paths at the point of the crossroads in this introduction, Aidoo illustrates Ato's state of double consciousness and foreshadows future events.

While the introduction sets up the dilemma, with the graduation scene, Aidoo suggests that Ato is already leaning towards a certain path. Obviously, influenced by Western culture, Ato, the expected bachelor and traditional son, is already married. Ato's decision to marry without the knowledge of his family was a complete disregard for his culture since marriage is a communal affair that his uncles have to handle and not he alone. Moreover, marrying an outsider, a wayfarer, someone without a tribe (11), obviously denotes he is not operating from an African (Akan) cultural consciousness. This diversion from his culture is further substantiated when he opts to practice birth control.

> 'Lalie, don't you believe me when I tell you its O.K.? I love you, Eulalie and that's what matters. Your own sweet self should be O.K. for any guy. And how can a first born be difficult to please? Children, who wants them? In fact, they will make me jealous. I couldn't bear seeing you love someone else better than you do me. Not yet, darling, and not even my own children.' (4)

From a Western perspective, what Ato says here may not be problematic, but in his cultural context, it is unacceptable.

48

To question the desire for children may sound insane to a people who hold that a '"woman's role as a wife is secondary to her role as mother,"' a people who measure a woman's worth by how many (male) children she has (Wilentz 54). But that Ato appears to ascribe to Western culture is not the entire problem posed in the text. Ato promotes discord with his wife and family when he hides behind his decisions. He obviously wants to live what might be a more liberated life. This would be a life that does not restrict but offers other possibilities not granted in a traditional African lifestyle. It can be an attempt to find a place for oneself, a place where he and Eulalie can live without being confronted about the choices they make. But because Ato is still uncertain about what a liberated life entails and is not prepared for cultural/communal criticism, he consistently hides behind a veil (Du Bois). This contributes to the state of confusion that lends to a criticism of Ato as Du Bois' confused "double-self," being both/and neither (Wilentz 54).

But it is also at this state of being a double-self, both/and neither that Ato is able to hide from his family's confronting questions. In order to avoid any one sense of responsibility, the double self becomes a form of resistance. But with this resistance, Aidoo demonstrates with the children's play and Ato's dream that he and Eulalie are caught in a childlike state. The girl and boy represent the superficiality of their characters, their uncertainty of themselves and their direction. Eulalie, like many Diaspora Africans, holds a false romanticized notion about her "native" land and the people. But Ato, the "native boy," seems to be more lost than his wife is. Eulalie acts often out of ignorance; Ato however acts refusing to acknowledge and attend to the issues threatening his marital and familial relationships. For instance, in the episode with the children, the boy hits the girl for wanting to assert a choice in their game. The exchange foreshadows Ato and Eulalie's discord. When Eulalie confronts Ato about her victimization as a result of his dishonesty, like the boy, he resorts to violence. This is a climatic scene because here, Eulalie refuses to continue Ato's lie. Her decision threatens to expose his pretensions and façade. In so doing, Eulalie reclaims herself from his manipulation. At this point, it appears that Ato would be forced to make a decision, but as revealed at the end of the work, he is still confronted with the dilemma. Reading Ato against Althusser, Odamtten confirms the Du Boisian analysis by asserting that Ato is indeed "a sujet-en-soi."

According to Odamtten, Ato lacks "critical self-consciousness that allows him as a subject to grasp fully the nature of his conditioning by different and conflicting ideological practices or discourses...he does not want to be reminded of his "other" self, that self that his traditional upbringing has shaped" (32-33 & 34). And because Ato is struggling with this duality and seems incapable of asserting a position or a reinventing of himself, he is the same at the end of the work as he was at the beginning. This confused been-to is yet to develop as a strong character.

Anowa, Aidoo's second play is set during the colonial era. The play addresses Africa's role in the slave trade as well as re-presents the legend of the resistant and independent girl who, not taking the advice of her parents, comes to a tragic end. By depicting Anowa as a subversive and vocal woman of this era, Aidoo attempts to break the silence that Ghanaians and Africans in general have imposed on the matter of the slave trade. In so doing, as a writer against (neo)colonialism, she illustrates how Africans, enticed by capitalistic greed and European ideals turn to subordinate their own people. Aidoo does with *Anowa* what Byron

Caminero-Santangelo argues Ngugi does with *A Grain of Wheat* that, "*A Grain of Wheat* strives to unlink a particular national or racial identity ('British') from a particular repressive form of governance ('colonialism')" (144). While Ngugi's novel is of the postcolonial era, writing against neo- colonialism, Aidoo's *Anowa*, though situated in colonial times, warns against Africans' exploitation of their own kind. As history informs, slavery in Africa did not begin with the European contact but had been a practice centuries before. By broaching Africa's participation in the business of slavery and also the transatlantic slave trade, Aidoo addresses that painful exploitative history. With a mention of the bond of 1844, which was the document officiating British colonial rule in what they called the Gold Coast, colonial decorations and a picture of Queen Victoria in Kofi's Big House (43), the play presents the effects of the colonial enterprise on the people.

With the character of Kofi Ako, Aidoo demonstrates one of the dangers of colonialism. Once a victim, a person *othered* first by the European and second by his community where he is marginalised, Kofi Ako desires to sit in the master's house. According to Badua, he is a lazy boy without future prospects. He also does not fit the positive image of a man as his masculinity is questioned. It is this marginalisation which in part prompts Kofi and Anowa to leave Yebi and make a new life elsewhere. But with the beginning of their prosperity, which is largely due to his hard working wife, Kofi begins to move into a role that insists on the oppression of others. Caminero- Santangelo observes that minorities who "advance materially and politically at the expense of the rest of the 'nation'" actually "become part of the first world which benefits from the underdevelopment of the third world..." (145). Kofi disregards the humanity of others so that he might be elevated in the community.

Against Anowa's wishes, Kofi decides to "deal in slaves" to acquire his wealth. He says, "now here is something I am going to do whether you like it or not. I do not even understand why you want to make so much noise about something like this. What is wrong with buying one or two people to help us? They are cheap...Every one does it...does not everyone do it?" (29-30). Anowa's response is: "Kofi, no man made a slave of his friend and came to much himself. It is wrong. It is evil" (30). As Fanon would argue, it is out of the need to be recognized as successful after being discounted and marginalised that Kofi embarks on a new life at the expense of others. Because success here is determined by one's economic and social position, the highest form of success and prestige that one may attain is that enjoyed by the Master. In colonial Africa, it becomes a matter of acquiring slaves, a Big House and living at the same exploitative level as the settlers. Carole Boyce Davies discusses the symbolic meaning attached to the Big House. She says that "the Big House" is an external reference for the entrenchment of colonial power and male dominance" (61). Furthermore, relating Kofi's Big House to Jody Starks' in Hurston's *Their Eyes Were Watching God*, she explains that the Big House "is a common staple of African and Caribbean anti-colonial literature" for it is "the sign of the colonised male's entitlement and concomitant female disempowerment" (66).

In her position against Kofi, Anowa expresses an understanding of the harm involved with the subjugation of a people, the separation from their families and the forced labour they perform. But while the slaves are forced to endure an inhumane life, Anowa also acknowledges that it strips the coloniser of his humanity. The old man also comments on Anowa and Kofi's venture. Critiquing the capitalistic greed that leads Kofi to enslave others, he says, "...money making is like a god possessing a priest. He never will leave, until he has occupied you, wholly changed the order of your being and seared you through and up and down." (39). Anowa's and the old man's words echo Cesaire's. Cesaire maintains that colonization works to de- civilise, brutalise, degrade the coloniser and awakens him to buried instincts of covetousness and violence (13). Here, Sissie's epiphany confirms Cesaire's point, but Aidoo reveals there is a price that comes with the exploitation of humanity. In Kofi's case, it results in his impotence, embarrassment and suicide.

Before Kofi's demise, we witness a heightened level of self-denial through an excessive imitation of European life. At this point, because of his success in exportation, he is known as possibly the richest man in the entire coast of Guinea (44). Although there is no mention of Kofi's connection to royalty in Yebi, and considering that he has moved into another town, Kofi acquires enough money that he is made a chief in Oguaa. That Kofi becomes a chief is noteworthy, for there is a peculiar desperation in him to attain a new identity. Upon his entrance into his Big House, which is decorated with the most elaborate and "consciously foreign articles" (43), Kofi is treated like a chief. He is "borne by four brawny men in a carrier chair. He is resplendent in brilliant Kente or velvet cloth and he is over-flowing with gold jewellery, from the crown of his head to the rings of his toes. He is surrounded by women and an orchestra of horns and drums. As he passes, he makes gestures of lordship over the area" (44).

Like the master/coloniser, Kofi claims the bodies and lives of African people in order to obtain his privileged position. Aidoo reveals the disturbed moral state of these colonised subjects as Kofi's means are not criticised but rather celebrated because of the wealth he has accumulated. Furthermore, while Kofi has separated himself from Yebi and also his family, he nevertheless seems to be holding on to his past. A look at his house indicates that he has not completely divorced himself from his background since there is a large painting of the crow, the totem bird of the Nsona clan on display (43). That Kofi has the symbol of the clan in his house and is presenting himself as a chief in another town is confused. Aidoo does not inform that the royal clan in Oguaa is Nsona. This is a possibility, but even if the people are members of the Nsona family, because Oguaa is not Kofi's home, he is not likely to have any royal authority in that space. Secondly, if the royal clan of Oguaa is not Nsona, Kofi's display of the bird suggests an attempt to yield some sort of significance or power when it is in fact insignificant to his acquired chieftaincy. Honouring his own clan while serving as an (honorary) chief in another appears to be a confused claim for dual identity. If the royal clan is not Nsona, then Kofi's display of the clan's symbol in his home is pointless since it can only serve as a form of paraphernalia and nothing else. It is possible that there is no effect in the symbol just as there might not be one in his title as chief.

Kofi's new identity as Master and Chief proposes an ambiguous and complicated relationship with his colonisers and people. His assumed position as a wealthy Master and possessor of black bodies is a replication of England's role in slavery and colonization. By engaging in this activity, Kofi becomes one with the dominant power. With the description of the intricate details in the Big House, Aidoo reveals Kofi's illusions of his acquired power and identity. Besides the expensive foreign furniture, the arrangement of the house speaks of an imitation of an affluent European home as might be pictured in a magazine. For instance, the narrator's reference to a fireplace in the central wall of the living room indicates this forced imitation. The fireplace again suspiciously appears as an attempted duplication of European lifestyle since there is no clear reason for Kofi to need a fireplace in a country with such a hot climate. Kofi's fireplace is therefore a form of decoration, a symbolic connection to a European life. Also, above the fireplace is a picture of Queen Victoria and to the left of the picture is one of Kofi himself. Note that his wife Anowa's presence is not accounted for. The side by side pictures of the Queen and Kofi indicate an illusory marriage between the two. It is the queen's position or at least, that of a king that Kofi yearns for. And because these goals are clearly beyond his reach, his only alternative is to pretend that he is somehow personally connected to the Queen. Moreover, the symbolic presence of the queen speaks to Kofi's endorsement of colonialism as a legitimate means of acquiring wealth and status. Aidoo further elaborates on this idea when Anowa recalls her dream and conversation with her grandmother immediately after Kofi and his Big House are introduced. It is here that an explicit connection is made with Kofi and Europeans. The discussion about the big houses built by whites, a reference to the slave castles, points to Kofi's repetition of a painful history of his people. It is with this portrayal of Kofi Ako that Aidoo writes against colonialism.

Further stressing the trouble associated with the need to be empowered through others' domination, Aidoo explores the relationship between Kofi and Anowa. Boyce Davies maintains that "Kofi's need to assert his masculinity, and thus achieve full acceptance in his community hinges both on oppressing others in slave labour and on subordinating the female" (*Black Women, Writing* 71). Because his maleness and sexuality are challenged, he attempts to escape from the stigma of the impotent and questionable male and embody what he and his society consider masculine. Deciding to reconstruct himself as the "new man," he takes the appearance of a strong male as a result of his wealth, slaves and titles. To complete this image of ultimate manhood, he subordinates his wife. He says, "Anowa truly has a few strong ideas. But I know she will settle down. Anowa, I shall be the new husband and you the new wife" (27). Kofi's means of domination is to repress Anowa's voice because her silence awards him alone with the right to speak and uphold an undisputed presentation of manhood and power. To escape Yebi's characterisation of him as a weak man, a watery cassava man, a description which lends to an interpretation of Kofi as a possible closeted homosexual, (*Black Women, Writing* 72) he must reinvent himself. Hence, this reinvention requires he possess power to exploit others.

With Aidoo's latest novel *Changes: A Love Story*, we move from a colonial era into a neo-colonial one. The major male character, Ali Kondey, is also a member of Ghana's elite. Because Ali grew up during the latter days of colonialism, he is a beneficiary of the independence struggles and opportunities offered by his new government. With an impressive educational background (beginning in Ghana and ending in England) and following his father's footsteps as a prominent businessman, Ali establishes a lucrative travel agency with various branches in Ghana and neighbouring countries (24). Like Kofi Ako, to Ali, becoming a member of the elite implies securing a privileged role. So although he is mainly presented in the novel as a rich and handsome lover, because of how he situates himself as a result of his education, wealth and physical appearance, Ali's character lends itself to a reading against neo-colonialism.

Aidoo tells us early in the text that "Ali was a son of the world" (22). He claimed the entire Guinea Coast, its hinterland and the Sub-Sahel for his own. Because his "grandfather's house had stood on the exact spot where Burkina Faso, Ghana and Togo met," and also that his father, Musa Musa, a trader, had travelled in these areas, "he [Ali] had assumed the nationalities of Ghana, Benin, Cote d'Ivoire, Burkina Faso, Niger, Mali, Nigeria and Togo." Ali boasted of his entitlement to them. "Naturally, he carried a passport to prove the genuineness of each" (23-24). Ali's claim to all these parts is arguable, but what is disturbing is the arrogance that accompanies his declaration of entitlement. He relies on this information to elevate himself in the company of others, especially women, as he casually imparts it as part of his description and resume in his pursuit of them. Ali approaches these nations as pieces of land and cultures that he can easily grant himself. In so doing, he plays the role of the coloniser who effortlessly lands in indigenous nations and claims them as his own.

Ali's colonisation does not end in Africa but extends to European countries. A wealthy and elite African neo-colonial, he frequently travels around the world. In these different spaces, he helps himself to precious materials, textiles, artefacts and exotic foods. He buys gold bangles from the Gulf States and succulent dates from Algeria. He brings huge slabs of chocolates from Switzerland, gleaming copper things from Zambia and Zimbabwe, shimmering silk from China, the Koreas and Thailand. From the Soviet Union, he buys special amber- inlaid wrought iron jewellery, electronics from Japan and from other advanced countries, ethnic goods and local crafts. By bringing all these gifts to his family, Esi feels she "saw the entire world from her little bungalow" (157-158). Undoubtedly, Aidoo is pointing to Ali's relationship to these countries because her list and discussion of his elaborate purchases are covered in detail. Although it is common and expected for one to purchase and acquire souvenirs from his travels, this excessive display by Ali, "a citizen of the world," is nevertheless a direct exploitation of individual nations and cultures. Ali's exploitation of other people is not a result of a sense of inferiority as it is with Kofi, rather, we see Ali more as a migrating figure perpetually on a mission. As noted above, his migrations to other countries result in their exploitation. It is perhaps safe to say that by showing how he can easily purchase and acquire pieces of a people's lives and identity, Ali is identifying himself with the coloniser who Cesaire calls an adventurer and a wholesale grocer (10). By undertaking this role, it can be inferred that Ali rationalises that his wealth and elite status entitle him to these things. Such rationalisation is not far from the coloniser believing that it was the privilege of his race that allowed him dominance over others.

Keeping to his role as coloniser, Ali easily claims the bodies of black women. The novel begins with Ali having one wife and, in the end, he manages to acquire another wife and a concubine, three women in all. It is Ali's cavalier dealings with women that cause Maria Olaussen to posit that Esi's sexuality becomes a commodity controlled by Ali ("About Lovers" 62). A polygamist and pseudo traditionalist, Ali enjoys the benefits provided him by his culture and religion. While Ali is supposedly content in his marriage and life with Fusena, he decides to make Esi his second wife. When Esi questions if it is not bigamy, Ali grows upset and responds:

[w]hen you put it like that, yes, we are committing a crime. Polygamy, bigamy. To the people who created the concepts, these are all crimes. Like homicide, rape and arson. Why have we got so used to describing our cultural dynamics with the condemnatory tone of our masters' voices? We have got marriage in Africa, Esi...And in our marriages a man has a choice -to have one or more wives....As long as he can look after them properly. (90)

Here, Ali makes a grand stand presenting himself as if an authority on the social and intricate details of custom. Indeed it is in his right to have several wives as a Moslem and an African man, but it becomes apparent that Ali is not exactly knowledgeable about this tradition and the procedures he should follow in regard to this "right." Without consulting any member of his family, he engages Esi and attempts to proceed with the marriage ceremony. After going to Esi's village without the proper companions, he is embarrassed and sent away. Ali's inconsiderate and spontaneous actions reveal that while he presents himself as an authority on the subject, he is ignorant of his own culture. Through his self-centred acts, we see that he simply wants to enjoy the benefits of polygamy and not necessarily honour the tradition or the people involved. Thus, for Ali, women can be easily had as the goods he brings from abroad. This is further demonstrated within the text when he initiates another affair with his secretary while maintaining his wives with gifts in place of his love, attention and presence. Olaussen is right when she observes that with Ali's and Esi's relationship, "the choice is finally not between monogamy or polygamy, 'Western,' "traditional' or Islamic marriages, but between oppressive, exploitative, and alienating arrangements that serve to further social control…" (72). Both Esi and Fusena find themselves unsatisfied and deceived by Ali. His quest for status and unlimited freedom infringes, disregards and overshadows theirs. Ali's relationship with these women requires that he be the dominant party and they the subordinate. It mirrors the relationship of the coloniser and the colonised. Ama Ata Aidoo carefully presents three very different men who speak to the effects of colonial and masculinist exploitation. Aidoo portrays through these works the importance of writing against neo-colonialism, demonstrating the negative impacts on the psyche of the colonised, his family and nation.

Chapter Four

Marriage and Fatherhood Stories

W.Agorde

> In our culture, and most others as well, women bear most of the burdens involved in childcare and houseworkthe work necessary to keep a household togetherwhile men carry a larger share of the authority and decision-making power within the family. [. . .] "Women's work" has traditionally been work within the home, while men have traditionally had far more freedom to indulge in cultural and intellectual pursuits. (Wolf 128)

GHANAIAN society clearly distinguishes the role and position of males and females because of the institutionalised responsibilities prescribed for both adult males and females. Although the position of women have changed within the past couple of decades, it is still evident that Ghanaian society is a man's world where majority of women are relegated to the domestic arena as mothers, cooks, and house cleaners. Men occupy positions of authority and respect in many spheres of society, but not all males attain full masculinity: Ghanaian society regards some males as "man-woman". A man may actually be called a woman or described as not a man at all. Many writers have observed that, in many societies, a person born with a penis does not automatically gain access to

60

masculinity; he must earn it by performing certain prescribed acts (Connell; Gilmore; Kimmel & Aronson; Nock). Nock notes that "masculinity is more than an attribute that males possess automatically by virtue of their anatomy, age, or maturation; rather, it is something that must be attained or earned" (43). Masculinity would appear to be a demand placed on men even if they do not want it; males are expected to become sufficiently masculine before they receive the full right to become members of the adult society. Those who do not conform to their society's demands suffer various consequences ranging from private or public ridicule to exclusion from certain jobs or clubs (Nock 43, 49). The test for manhood "is found at all levels of socio-cultural development regardless of what other alternative roles are recognized. It is found among the simplest hunters and fishermen, among peasants and sophisticated urbanized peoples; it is found in all continents and environments" (Gilmore 11). Every society, irrespective of social structure, societal norms, or economic or political affiliations requires that men prove their manhood.

Male children in Ghanaian society have prescribed acts to perform in order to participate in the masculine culture. Irrespective of one's tribe, language, geographical location or class, Ghanaian boys are expected to grow from boyhood to manhood and this evolution does not depend on age only. To become an adult, both boys and girls are taken through initiation rites that introduce them to adulthood. Sarpong records that "[a]fter the performance of one's initiation ceremonies, one has the right and at times bound, to perform certain acts that were formerly out of bounds to one" (73). Initiation rites announce that a young person has been promoted from childhood to adulthood. Upon reaching the latter stage, society demands the performance of certain

61

undertakings that will give recognition to the new adult. One of the most important requirements after initiation rites is marriage. Ghanaians believe that, apart from the days of birth and death, the day of marriage is the most important in a person's life. Gyekye draws attention to the importance of marriage, especially to men:

> Marriage is a requirement of the society, an obligation every man and woman must fulfil, a drama of life in which every man and woman must participate [. . .] a young man who has gainful employment of any kind and earns income is expected, in fact urged to marry. Any undue delay on part of the young man to marry will cause his parents or the elders in the lineage to worry and even to interfere in his private life in order to advise and encourage him to marry. (76)

Using theories of men and masculinities with selected Ghanaian video films, this article carefully examines the importance of marriage and fatherhood in both traditional and urban Ghanaian societies as processes of men asserting their masculinities. It traces the position of fathers in the rural areas and different types of fatherhood practices in urban dwelling communities.

Family Drama

The production of low budget video films started in Ghana in 1987 resulting in the release of many video films in English and local languages. The emergence of the video film tradition became necessary when the state-owned Ghana Film Industry Corporation (GFIC) could not produce films due to lack of funds. The tradition of video film production started with people who had no training in the art of film making. Their lack of professional training is manifested in the way

62

conventions regarding script writing, theme, and overall message were not given any professional attention. In addition, technical issues were ignored as the films were shot with ordinary super-VHS cameras with most feature films shot within one to three weeks on a budget of $5000 to $15000. In order to cut down cost of production, many producers wrote the scripts, directed the production, and played the lead role in the film. The scripts written were brief outlines which usually left room for actors to improvise on the story. Majority of the actors involved in the productions have no professional training in acting so they do it simply for their love for acting while others are excited to appear on television. In spite of the imperfection of these films and the visible technical flaws that are very conspicuous, they are box office hits and they compete with foreign films from North America, Asia, and Europe. As more video films were produced most cinema houses in the big cities like Accra, Kumasi and Takoradi showed less foreign movies; weekends and holidays were solely reserved for the screening of Ghanaian movies. Meyer observes that "the emergence of video technology clearly marked the beginning of a mass media revolution which made it increasingly difficult for the nation state to control the consumption of images by its subjects"(*Popular Ghanaian*, 5).

Family drama has dominated the Ghanaian video scene since its inception. These movies explore the problems that confront people at home as they are usually set in the house of the main protagonists. There is a distinct demarcation between the houses in the urban centres and those of the rural areas: houses in the cities are walled and there is a huge iron gate which is usually guarded by a security man. These houses are occupied by the modern nuclear family. The fence separates the nuclear family members from the extended family.

Houses in the rural areas are usually without walls or even if they have walls, they are such that people can easily move to and from the houses without much interference. The free movement of people in the rural areas promotes the sense of community. Meyer explains that "[f]ocusing on marital drama, with all the conflicts between the spouses and the extended family it entails, popular films highlight problems that are easily recognizable to the audiences" ("Ghanaian Popular Cinema", 212). The popular use of domestic space could also be the fact that marriage is one of the most important institutions among Ghanaians; they consider the family as the bedrock on which society thrives.

The Role of Men in Marriage

Nock identifies three main areas where fathers are expected to function in the family: "(1) Fathers to their wives' children; (2) providers for their families and (3) protectors of their wives and children" (50). Contemporary video films whether set in rural or urban communities, project married men in the process of performing the above three roles. The performance of these roles differs largely depending on a man's geographical location, economic conditions, and level of education. As Nock outlines, marriage puts a man in a privileged position in society, therefore, he is expected to consistently affirm, reaffirm, and validate his masculinity:

> The young husband is a different social and legal person than he was as a bachelor. He is held to different standards. He is accorded different treatment by friends, family, associates, and strangers. He may legitimately claim greater autonomy and respect than before he

64

married. He has, made a public commitment of the most enduring and binding sort. He expects to be treated as mature, stable, productive, and dependable. (52)

A young man who gets married is respected in Ghanaian society hence it is required that he is adequately prepared both psychologically and economically before he enters marriage.

Tribal War 1 & 2

Tribal War is a two-part movie which explores the bucolic life of Efo and Koo Kuma's families. Efo and Koo Kuma both heads of the Ewe and Ashanti families respectively decide to pursue a serious enmity that exists between the two families. The origin of the contention which is based on tribal affiliation is not known to the families. They decide to nurture their hatred for each other because their forebears were enemies. Koo Kuma swears never to have anything to do with Efo and his family and Ewes in general. Efo also severely warns his family never to go near Koo Kuma or members of his tribe. The hatred for each other is so intense that whenever members of both families meet, they either physically or verbally assault each other. Unfortunately, Owusu, the first son of Koo Kuma, falls in love with Enyo, Efo's elder daughter. The lovers, aware of the consequences of their relationship, resort to unorthodox means to keep their love a secret. With time, Efo suspects that Enyo is in a relationship with someone from Koo Kuma's family. Lebene, Enyo's elder brother, is instructed to monitor Enyo's movements. When the secret of the lovers is discovered, Koo Kuma vows to kill Owusu while Efo locks Enyo in a room after ruthlessly beating her. Owusu manages to release Enyo from her house arrest and both elope to Kumasi.

After living in the city for twelve years and becoming successful business couple they decide to return to the village with their daughter Dzifa.

Fatherhood in the Rural World

The setting of *Tribal War* presents the Ghanaian bucolic lifestyle where in male-headed households form the foundation of society and determines how family life operates. As heads of their respective households Efo and Koo Kuma serve as the spiritual and political representatives of their families and exercise absolute authority over their wives and children. These fathers are powerful figures in the family who gain authority from agricultural exploits because farming is the main income-generating activity for the family. Every member of the family actively participates in farming to make economic contributions for the survival of the family. Efo and Koo Kuma rule their families with strict rules and regulations; anyone who thinks contrary to their thought process is branded a betrayer of the family. The fathers gain authority over the family as a result of being the owners of the family land and family business. Both characters' initial placement in the movie is in the bush, a place connected to their main source of livelihood, therefore their initial appearance establishes their position as authority figures. With the produce they gather from the farm, Efo and Koo Kuma feed their families and as a result are able to exert complete control over their families. Rotundo identifies that the power of the father is connected to his ownership and control of all family property because "[t]hrough his control of land, a father could direct the rate at which his son's gained their independence" (65-66).

Efo's son, Lebene, and Koo Kuma's sons, Owusu and Bota, are directly under the control of their respective fathers. Owusu does not agree with the family feud with Efo's family but he cannot challenge his father. Due to the conflict in both families it is impossible for him to make his love to Enyo known to either family because he is aware Koo Kuma will violently oppose the proposal.Bota and Lebene are the favourites of their respective fathers because they support their fathers in everything regardless to whether it is good or bad. None of the boys in both families could gain their independence without their fathers' permission. The fathers monitor their sons by influencing the economic activities they engage in and the people they associate with. The boys could not select their own marriage partners without their fathers' consent. Even after marriage Lebene and .Bota continue to reside in the family house with their parents. The continuous stay of these boys in the family house makes them incapable of taking charge of their lives and validating their masculinities. They do not have control over their immediate families because their fathers interfere with the way they relate to their wives. Bota and Lebene are neither independent nor heads of their households because they are answerable to their fathers and therefore, occupy subordinate masculine positions. Efo and Koo Kuma use their sons to validate their (fathers) hegemonic masculine positions. Both fathers' attitude and control over their families is compatible with Scott Coltrane's description of the pre-industrial family home which "was […] a system of control, as well as a centre of production, and both functions reinforced the father's authority and shaped family relationships" (270).

As a further control mechanism, fathers are directly involved in the training of their sons so Bota and Lebene continue working with their fathers even after marriage.

Griswold notes that "rural living meant that fathers lived and worked in close proximity to their children. In rural areas, men helped organize the work of the household and introduced sons to the ways and rhythms of farm life;..." (161). Bota works with Koo Kuma as blacksmith and Lebene works with Efo in hunting and farming. It is rather difficult to differentiate between childhood and adulthood for Bota and Lebene since their lives and conditions do not change after they marry and produce children. Their fathers still manipulate them since they do not own any economic activity for themselves. It is impossible for these boys to achieve their own masculine status in their fathers' presence. Lebene and Bota cannot maintain their marriages because they are rendered impotent as far as family authority and decision making are concerned. Whiles the presence of Bota and Lebene in the family enhances the image of their fathers, the boys suffer serious retrogression in the development of their masculine status. Because fathers are solely responsible for ushering their sons into manhood, any undue delay on the part of the fathers adversely affects the children. Bota becomes an object of scorn before his wife as Koo Kuma still maintains absolute control over him.

Nock explains that marriage "is associated with notions of maturity and thus confers some amount of legitimacy to such a claim. In their married roles as fathers, providers, and protectors, husbands validate themselves as mature men" (56). Efo and Koo Kuma are successful fathers who perform their breadwinner roles effectively. Family security and economic stability are their major focus. They construct their unique masculinities by working hard on the farm and providing the family's immediate needs. These fathers are towering figures in their families so they have absolute control over their children and have the responsibility of ensuring their growth and development into responsible adults. Koo Kuma and Efo believe it is their duty to train their children to hate Ashantis and Ewes respectively. Both fathers, on several occasions, explain to their families the reasons why they must hate the other tribe. In that instance, hatred, bitterness, tribalism and nepotism are transmitted into the children. This is a disturbing nature of the father figure in the rural world. Since their power is absolute and they are not answerable to anyone, it is difficult to challenge them even when their children do not agree with their beliefs. The father's absolute rights in the family cause devastating emotional and physical torture.

One notable nature of father's right John Stoltenberg identifies "is the quality of violence required to enforce it, the quality of violence required to perpetuate it, to keep it the form which humans live out their lives, the air they breathe so long as they inhale and exhale" (54). The family becomes a site for oppression of children and women. Efo demonstrates his dominion over the family through violence and intimidation. He tells Lebene how he (Efo) has tamed his wife and encourages Lebene to do likewise. Efo's wife is reduced to the position of a domestic servant who is always poised to do the commands of her husband. Her thoughts and ideas are not considered important. She is responsible for raising their two daughters, however, the girls are raised according to Efo's demands and expectations. Her domestic responsibilities are carried out the way Efo outlines. Nukunya elucidates that "[t]he marital relationship is marked by the complete obedience of the wife. Every wife is expected to obey her husband. He may beat her for disobedience, disorderliness and any suspicion of unfaithfulness" (155). John M. Clum commenting on the patriarchal family also remarks that it is "structured on the notion of family hierarchy as the basis of gender order. However immature the patriarch may appear, however out of touch he seems in the domestic economy, his pre-eminent place is unquestioned, and women need to adapt to their secondary position" (25). When Efo discovers Enyo's secret love affair, he blames his wife for training the girls wrongly. He accuses his wife for not being a good mother to the daughters. The woman is required to perform her subordinate role satisfactorily in order to enhance Efo's superior image as a responsible father. He is proud of Lebene who obeys him by being violent towards the girls and Koo Kuma's family. Efo believes that his son and daughters occupy separate spheres in life thereby need to be treated differently. Michele Adams and Scott Coltrane note that:

> although cross cultural variation in the actual content of gender roles is enormous, families generally teach us that women and men should occupy different places in the social order, relying on the ideology of separate spheres, families continue to raise children "to be" masculine or feminine based on the reproductive equipment with which they are born. (232)

Enyo and her sister are destined to be the keepers of the home while Lebene belongs to the public space. In Efo's family, the consequence of crossing the gender boundary is tantamount to negative ramifications which are usually blamed on his wife. The separate spheres ideology also promotes men into the position of authority whiles women remain subordinates. The traditional family provides the environment where "men continued to exercise power and control over women sexually, socially, and physically, though often under the name of a religiously sanctioned paternal authority" (Adams & Coltrane 240). Even Lebene and Bota who play subordinate masculine roles in their respective homes believe it is their right as husbands to control their wives. Efo and Koo Kuma accuse their male children of being weak because the boys do not use violence and intimidation to control their wives.

Koo Kuma and Efo believe that women are properties who must be controlled and suppressed at every possible opportunity. They act as if women do not have a mind of their own but are owned by their husbands. Stoltenberg explains the process of male ownership as follows:

> The reality of male ownership in all human relationships under father right can be seen immediately and most clearly as it affects the lives of humans defined by all culture as femaleall humans, that is, who were born without a penis. At no time in a woman's life is she not defined by law and culture as the actual or potential property of someone who is male, someone born with a penis.
> First, as a child, she is owned by a father, the man who owns the flesh of her mother in marriage. That man owns her as daughter until such a time she is possessed carnally and legally by a husband. (55)

Among every Ghanaian society a man pays dowry in order to get a woman's hand in marriage. Though there are differences from one ethnic group to the other, generally men offer drinks, money and other gifts. Nukunya notes that "[t]hroughout Ghana, and indeed sub-Saharan Africa as a whole, women are traditionally given in marriage through the initiative of their parents, sometimes without their consent, or even knowledge of their future husbands" (41). The bride price makes men like Efo, Lebene, Koo Kuma and Bota consider their wives as properties. When Lebene's wife threaten to leave the marriage, Lebene gives a sarcastic laugh because he believes the woman is nothing without him so she cannot take a decision on her own and successfully execute it. Stoltenberg is correct when he further notes that "[t]o this day, the marriage ceremony is a ritual reminder that title to a woman's body has been transferred from one male owner to another" (55). In the traditional society, girls have very little to say as far as the choice of their spouses are concerned. A girl who refuses to accept a man's hand in marriage is considered rebellious and thereby deserving of punishment. The towering father figure from the rural area is transferred to certain fatherhood practices in the city as projected in *A Call at Midnight*.

The Modern Father as Protector

Beside the breadwinner role, fathers also serve as protectors of the families. Many fathers with teenage or unmarried adult daughters are very concerned about their daughters' relationship with the opposite sex. They usually play their protective role as a means of asserting their masculinities and usurping their authority at home. When Simon gets to know that Titus is dating his (Simon's) daughter, Sama, he gets angry and physically assaults Titus and in addition, he withholds certain privileges that Titus deserves as a worker in the company. This confirms Nock's assertion that fathers are expected to be protectors of their children and wives. They are required to stand for the family by defending it through courage as well as being loyal to the family (50). Nevertheless, Simon exhibits a kind of protection that is not only aimed at promoting the safety of his daughter but a means of asserting his hyper masculine status over Titus. Simon has serious issues to battle with as far as his daughter's relationship with Titus is concerned. Firstly, Titus is his subordinate at work and both have a strong proclivity for corruption and immorality, so Titus dating Sama is a threat to Simon since he will not like his daughter to be connected to a thief. He feels Titus deliberately decide to date Sama in order to test his (Simon) masculinity as such he thinks Titus does not respect him. Simon's masculinity is put to test by Titus and he must do everything to redeem his image. Simon crosses the line between private and public spaces by using his position in the public space to punish a private offence. Secondly, Simon is scared of his own immorality, therefore, he must keep his daughter away from unscrupulous men like himself. Though Simon is married he has a secret teenage girlfriend so he feels Titus may also use Sama and abandon her later. He knows that as a father, he is expected to be an example of good morality to his children but his inability to do so renders him vulnerable. He knows the consequences of dating teenagers therefore he must keep Titus away from Sama. Thirdly, his reaction to the relationship could also be a cover-up for his inadequacies and lack of discipline. It is a means by which he takes attention from his own misdeeds. The over-reaction also points to the fact that, Simon is struggling to make up for his absence from home and lack of intimacy with his daughter. Besides fulfilling his breadwinner role, he has failed in many aspects of fatherhood and this opportunity creates the avenue for him to act and redeem his tarnished image.

In the plethora of video films produced over the years, it is evident that many fathers have lost touch of realities at home because they do not have any emotional attachment to their children. Teenage daughters especially are always under attack from their fathers because the fathers believe any man who gets near to their daughters is doing so with the sole aim of having sex with them. Instead of fathers like Simon playing the caring-counsellor-fatherly role, they take to hyper masculine tendencies that separate the family. Paul R. Amato's admonishes parents when he notes:

Parental control is harmful. [. . .] if it is enforced with coercive punishment, such as hitting. Furthermore, as children grow into adolescence, it is necessary for parents to relax their degree of regulation. If parents are too restrictive, adolescents do not have opportunities to develop new forms of competence, profit from their mistakes, and learn to accept responsibility for their own decisions. Excessive control may also generate feelings of resentment toward parents, thus eroding parent-child affection. Nevertheless, parental monitoring is still necessary to ensure that adolescents do well in school and do not drift into delinquent or antisocial activities. (245)

Simon does not succeed preventing Sama from being in love with Titus rather his (Simon's) hyper masculine instincts create impasse between him and his daughter hence Sama sees his father as an enemy. Such a father is a reproach to the family and his actions destabilises the family. Society expects fathers to have emotional attachment to their children as well as create a balance between work and family.

New Charismatic Fathers

There is a new form of fatherhood that is being played in the video films. These fathers consist of urban middle-class fathers who are actively involved in fathering and childcare. These new breed of fathers participate actively in the day-to-day lives of their children and they consider their wives as co-heads of the home. Rontundo refers to this new mode of fathering as "participant fatherhood". He describes the participant father as:

immersed in the tasks of day-to-day childcare. His wide ranging involvement flows from the assumption that after childbirth there

74

are few tasks that cannot be shared interchangeably by mother and father. But participant fatherhood means more than just fulfilling physical responsibilities to childrenit means intensive emotional involvement with them too. (74)

Odasani 1 & 2 provide a perfect picture of participant fatherhood. Mr. Bonsu and his wife Grace have three girls; the children are in their late teens and early twenties. Mr. Bonsu is a civil servant and Grace does petty trading. Mr. Bonsu takes a loan from his employers to enable him send his eldest daughter Erica for further studies abroad. Though Mr. Bonsu is solely responsible for the payment of the loan, he calls a family meeting to discuss the issue before taking the final decision. Bonsu discusses all major issues with his family before the plans are executed. When Erica travels abroad and sends money to help with family projects, Bonsu hands over the projects to Grace and makes her assume full responsibility over these projects. Bonsu always makes time to be with his family and he takes the family out regularly to dinners. He does not only provide physical amenities for the family but also connects with them emotionally. He serves as a channel of strength and hope in times of difficulties. He closely monitors his children's progress in school and when they write exams and pass to enter the university, he takes the family out to celebrate the children's success. Although Bonsu has a busy schedule at work, he consciously makes time to connect with the family at all times. His interaction with the family especially with the children is highly commendable. Communication in the family is very open as every issue is discussed in an atmosphere of peace. The Children of this home are a good example in their neighbourhood. Family time is used to discuss progressive issues rather than finding faults and addressing complains.

A major characteristic of the kind of fatherhood Bonsu displays revolves around his ability to treat his girls with the same level of attention that boys usually receive. Unlike Efo, in Tribal War, who believes in different spheres ideology, Bonsu does not leave raising the girls to Grace but he plays active role in every phase of their lives. Gender prescription and discrimination does not form part of Bonsu's fatherhood practices. Rotundo identifies that the blurring of gender division plays a key role in participant fatherhood because a man who practices this mode of fathering is required to avoid sex-role stereotypes in dealing with his children since "[h]e can encourage girls to be assertive achievers, and he can coach daughters as well as sons in competitive sports". The new model of fatherhood Rontundo further notes "demands new pattern of feeling; it entails different notions of male and female; and it requires men to surrender substantial authority to their wives in return for a greater measure of involvement with their children" (74-75). Bonus surrenders the family's economic base to Grace hence Grace becomes empowered to fully participate in the decision making process in the home.

Another example is Dr. Frank Addo's family in *Jennifer*. Frank is a father figure who is actively engaged with his daughter, Pricilla, of about ten years. He picks her from school and sometimes stays around with her to finish playing with her friends before he takes her home. He also cooks for himself and Pricilla whenever he finds the time. Pricilla and Frank spend quality times together playing games at home or at the park. Frank loves his daughter and he is determined to spend quality time with her but his job does not permit him to do so as much as he wants to. Frank's nurturing role is highly commendable but his job as a medical doctor takes him away from home most of the time. Also, Ken Omaboe in *Nightmare* believes in participatory fatherhood. Ken hurries to the hospital when he is informed that his wife is in labour. He stays by the woman to deliver. When his wife delivers he takes over shopping and buys the household needs and items necessary for childcare. However, Ken's wife is often seen alone with the baby because the man travels out of town on official duties.

How do men like Frank and Ken address the issue of being taken away from home during the time they are needed most? Although participant fatherhood seems to be an ideal model, it is only men who have flexible working hours that can afford spending a good deal of time at home. Other than that men can only get intensively involved in their role as fathers as a hobby because rigid work schedules do not permit men to be effective participant fathers. Unless there is a change in work schedules many fathers desiring to participate actively in the lives of their children will have to push their desire to the margins (Rotundo 77). It is necessary for the issue regarding work schedules to be well examined. Rontundo calls for a revision and new definition of working hours and jobs. Employers must revise and redefine paternal work schedules in order to give chance to fathers like Ken and Frank to spend time with their families. It is necessary for fathers to have adequate time to be with their preschool children. This will also call for a look at women's wage work. The point is, if women earn less than men and spend more time at home, fathers have no choice than to put in extra working hours in order to meet the family's financial needs.

From the illustrations in the video films, "breadwinning remains a key component of the father's roles in many, if not most, segments of society today. . ." (Lamb 50). Male characters like Simon, Mr. Ansah, Peterson, Chief Robertson, and Chief Johnson in various Ghanaian video films can give excuses of spending less time at home because they have to work hard and support their families since their wives are housewives. Kwamina Simon for example hardly gets any time for the family. The only time he gets any physical contact with her little daughter is when the girl is asleep. It is difficult to accuse such fathers of being absent from home since they work extra hours to make enough money to sustain the family and supply all their needs. The strict division of labour at home privileges the man over the woman thereby making the man feel superior and as such he sees himself as "the woman's protector, and in this he is supported by the position allotted to women in the society at large" (Nukunya 155).

Conclusion

Fatherhood practices in Ghana have travelled a long way; men still have a lot of power in the home. Nevertheless, the situation keeps changing over the years. Women's labour and contribution towards the home is more recognised and appreciated in some homes now. Women's economic empowerment is necessary if there should be a change of trend in the authority in the home. Men still have so much authority because they still play their traditional breadwinner role. Some of them play the breadwinner role effectively but it gives them the excuse to be absent from home most of the time. Characters like Kwamina Simon use his work as an excuse to be an absent father. Such fathers do not have any emotional connection with their children hence they lack the needed skills to play their protective roles. When it comes to the issues of the security of the family, these men use the opportunity to exhibit their hyper masculine tendencies rather than fighting for the protection of the family. As the movies project, most of the urban middle-class men are loosing touch with the realities of issues at home. Children need to be connected to their fathers both physically and emotionally; these two ingredients are missing in many homes as far as men are concerned. When fathers think providing economically for the family is all they have to do, they fail to take care of other important matters that are not necessarily related to finances. Fathers must work hand-in-hand with their female partners in the training of children. The woman should not receive all the blame when something goes wrong whiles the man receives the victory plaque when everything is right. When fathers use the home as an arena for asserting their masculinities, they cause more harm than good.

Examining the pattern of fatherhood from the traditional fathers to the new charismatic fathers, it is obvious that many things have changed as far as the family structure is concerned. Throughout the patterns, economic factors play a major role in determining the kind of fatherhood that is played at a particular time. Examining the economic condition of the country and the images the video films portray, one cannot predict the future of fatherhood. Nevertheless, it will be a laudable venture to encourage more fathers to become participant fathers since that style of fatherhood positively affects many areas of the family structure. It is undeniable that men and women will continue to be parents hence the importance of creating the avenue for men to become participant fathers. There is the need for restructuring work schedules and women's wage work in order to make men like Frank Addo and Ken Omaboe to spend more time with their children. Fathers must take a queue from men like Mr. Bonsu who collapses gender binaries in their homes and give their daughters the same concentration and opportunity that the boy child enjoys.

Chapter Five

Postcolonial 'Writing Back'

A.Lewis

POST colonial literatures embody a dynamic of perpetually writing back in order to move forward, challenging misconceptions entrenched in and perpetuated by previous texts, whether on the basis of race, nationality, or gender, and opening fertile ground for future elaboration and discussion. In an attempt to forge an ever-widening space within the major critical discourses in the humanities, postcolonial literatures and theories engage in unlocking unspoken, unheard or silenced pasts (of individuals, communities, genders, nations) thus expanding the scope of possibility for culturally and politically viable presents and futures. Postcolonialism is primarily concerned with 'voicing'. Fundamentally, postcolonial literatures and theories aspire to the establishment of an ongoing dialogue, aiming to facilitate a "democratic colloquium between the antagonistic inheritors of the colonial aftermath" (Gandhi x). Inclusive rather than merely "nebulous" or "diffuse" (Gandhi viii), the dialogue of postcolonialism often focuses on regions "whose subjectivity has been constituted in part by the subordinating power of European colonialism" (Adam and Tiffin vii). The dialogue can also, on a wider level, mobilise "a set of discursive practices...[including] resistance to colonialism, colonialist ideologies" and their insidious contemporary forms and "subjectificatory legacies" (Adam and Tiffin vii). Indeed, this dialogue, or ongoing process of 'writing back', while situated in the symbolic and literary, is firmly engaged in the process of eliciting positive (and necessary) change in the real world. The explosion of Eurocentric notions of canonicity, literature, and language facilitates a

'decolonisation of the mind' of both African reading audiences and their white neo-colonial counterparts (wa Thiong'o).

This dynamic of writing back (and thus moving forward) is clearly visible in Chinua Achebe's *Things Fall Apart* (1958) and Tsitsi Dangarembga's *Ner vous Conditions* (1988). In this literary conversation, or argument, Joseph Conrad's Africanist images in *Heart of Darkness* (1917) provoke an impassioned response from Achebe, who in turn prompts Dangarembga to raise her voice. Dangarembga suggests that, in protesting the reductive 'othering' of the black African as 'savage' by skilfully portraying a rich and vivid pre-colonial Ibo existence, Achebe has effectively 'othered', or repressed the voices of, African women. The politics of writing in English, as well as the complex interplay between traditional and colonial forms of patriarchal oppression, will be explored as, departing from Spivak, it becomes apparent that it is not the case that 'the subaltern cannot speak', nor need the "babel" of subaltern voices be "unpleasant" or "confusing" (Gandhi 3). Rather, postcolonial texts such as *Things Fall Apart* and *Nervous Conditions* might most fruitfully be seen as speaking clearly and building with and upon each other in a process of self- assertion and self-empowerment, seeking not to have the definitive last word but rather to contribute to a multiplicity of voices, opinions and culturally-specific realities. Achebe and Dangarembga speak to Nigerian,

Zimbabwean, African and global audiences of past and present experiences (both positive and negative, 'traditional' and colonial) and thus pave the way, through greater awareness and respect for difference, to a positive future in an increasingly postcolonial world.

Set in much the same chronological period as *Heart of Darkness* (the late nineteenth century), *Things Fall Apart*, Achebe's response to Conrad's text, is an "object lesson" (Thieme 19) in how to achieve much-needed redefinition (and expression) of African subjectivities. Constructing an alternative fictional historiography of the incursion of European colonial society in West Africa, Achebe replaces the limited and reductive Eurocentric gaze with the deeper insights of an Ibo point of view. Achebe refrains from answering perceived racism with racism: his European characters, although heavily overlaid with ironic or symbolic commentary regarding white ignorance, are more three-dimensional than Conrad's 'natives', with the Reverend Smith's Manichaean worldview, where "black was evil", contrasted to his predecessor Mr Brown's more accommodating approach (TF 162). However, he presents the close-knit communities of Umuofia, and each of the Ibo individuals therein, as possessed of far greater agency, insight and interest than mere 'black shapes crouching' (HD 34). Ibo society is shown to be vibrant and complex. Fundamentally, Achebe deals the smug self-importance of empire a savage (harsh and calculated, not unthinkingly 'primitive'!) blow by displacing white missionaries, soldiers and government to the margins of the text. Their fatal imposition is registered, but it is only *part* of the text of African cultural history, with the first appearance of the colonialists, denaturalised through Ibo eyes as "albino" men (TF 121), not occurring until Chapter 15, a substantial way through the work.

In this sense, while Innes has claimed that Achebe "rarely lets his reader forget the otherness of the Igbo culture" (34), it is rather the case that the Western reader is 'othered' by the Ibo traditions and words which, while often explained in the glossary present in most editions, if not the text itself, act as a firm reminder that not all experience can be contained by the English language or the corresponding prevailing European worldview. From the Ibo perspective, cross-cultural encounters render the invaders ludicrous and lacking intelligence (rather than the reverse), a people who, in translation, seem unable to master the difference between "myself " and "my buttocks" (TF 126). As Obierika bitterly observes, it is unlikely that the white man will "understand our custom about land" when he "does not even speak our tongue" (TF 155). The dangers of cultural blindness and the self-legitimating superiority of the 'centre' are made starkly apparent in the sudden shift of perspective to the "the distant eyes of an outsider" (Harris 108) at the novel's close, where the striking juxtaposition in tone and insight betray the utter inadequacy of the uninvited, self-reflexive commentaries of the "student of primitive customs" (TF 182). The tragic hero Okonkwo (who, despite the masculinist orientation of his *chi,* or personal spirit, the reader has come to admire) is, in the District Commissioner's blinkered frame, nothing more than a limp body hanging from a tree: pacified, rather than staunchly resisting. The Commissioner concedes that the death of "one of the greatest men in Umuofia" is "interesting" enough to warrant "a reasonable paragraph" in his upcoming Africanist manual (TF 183). Achebe's work, as "Ur-text" of post-colonial African literary tradition, undermines this "rhetoric of lack" (Gikandi 8) by drawing attention to the need for whole books, by suitably qualified authors: Obierika would be such a spokesperson, had he not, like

Okonkwo, "choked" (TF 183) on his words in anger and frustration. As Huggan has suggested, while one of the greatest achievements of Achebe's "self-consciously hybrid" work is its success in attaching a local, largely ancestral, orally transmitted body of knowledge to an "imported sensibility, the modern European novel", he also manages to turn "the language of Western evolutionist anthropology against itself " (43). Not only does Achebe write back to a particular English canonical text, he also parodies "the whole of the discursive field" (Tiffin 23) within which such texts continue to operate, suggesting that, regardless of how "much thought" (TF 183) we devote to the critical enterprise, as long as a false sense of cultural superiority and Western self-definition against a 'primitive other' is maintained, the understandings produced will be fundamentally flawed.

Literary production is, for Achebe, a highly political act. In his view, art is not "pure", or removed from the context of its creation and reception, but should be actively "applied" to society in order to achieve positive "education" and change ("The Novelist As Teacher" cited in Osei-Nyame 148). Importantly, Achebe addresses an intended audience not only of white but, primarily, Nigerian readers, aiming to "teach...that their past...was not one long night of savagery from which the first Europeans acting on God's behalf delivered them" (148), and thus to restore a stolen "dignity" ("The Role of the Writer in a New Nation" cited in Ogungbesan 37) to the African postcolonial self-image.

Achebe asserts that the "world language...forced down our throats" by the history of colonisation (and continuing cultural imperialism) can be used, with skilful appropriation, as a "weapon of great strength" ("The African Writer and the English Language" 63): one with the potential to impact upon a wide reading audience. Although he hopes that the two hundred Nigerian mother tongues will continue to flourish (Rowell 262), Achebe envisages the gradual creation of "a new English" that can be made to "carry the weight of...African experience" ("The African Writer" 65), an idea which mirrors Bakhtin's conception of words being not only constrained by the traces of previous usages, but also open to the layering of new meanings that fit and validate different social and geographical demands and contexts (Harrow 27). In *Things Fall Apart*, Achebe succeeds in forging a written style that echoes oral story-telling, with an abundance of proverbs, "the palm-oil with which words are eaten" (TF 6), facilitating a heteroglossic orchestra of community voices that traverses past and present. The Yeatsian title and epigraph, appropriated from the Western canon, point to the devastation wreaked by empire-building practices as the imperial "knife" attacks the core values of its colonial peripheries, "the things that held us together" (TF 156); exposing, on another level, the fact that the 'heart of darkness', of human cruelty and despair, is not culturally specific but exists wherever "The best lack all conviction, while the worst/ Are full of passionate intensity" (W.B. Yeats, "The Second Coming"). However, African intertextualities and resonances are privileged in the text. As such the "straightforward act of bearing witness cracks" (Harrow 66), necessitating a slightly different mode of reading. Achebe paints a paradoxical portrait of a protagonist who is at once a

'typical' Ibo man (even an emblem or allegory of his entire society) and a selfish individualist (Nnoromele 152) who transgresses community values, transforming himself, in death, into an extended proverb or "warning...against taking too-rigid stances" (Harrow 67). As Okhamafe has observed, things begin to fall apart in the nine Umuofian villages long before white missionaries arrive (134), and the civil order crumbles largely because of internal stresses that lead the marginalised (including mothers of twins and osu (outcasts)) to "find relief outside" existing structures (Wren 35). This is not a simplistic acceptance of the "historical inevitability of modernization" on a linear frame à la Hegel (Booker 76) but a complex realisation of the "seemingly contradictory need for both tradition and transformation" (Harris 109), which can be applied with great effect to the contemporary setting, and the need to fashion an inclusive postcolonial order. We need to avoid equating 'tradition' with stasis, non-change, fixity.

As the world changes, and different voices jostle for attention, the process of writing back will necessarily be ongoing. Despite Achebe's successful illumination, subversion and explosion of the racial stereotypes of paradigmatic colonial texts, it has been suggested that, "for the modern woman writer in Africa," Achebe's (male) 'author-ity' must seem "as difficult to challenge as [was] the district commissioner's voice" in Achebe's time (Cobham 178). Much as Conrad repressed the perspectives of women excluding Kurtz's European 'Intended' from the domain of masculine reality and further sidelining his African mistress to the river bank several feminist critics contend that Achebe has relegated women to the margins, obscuring a valorisation of patriarchal domination beneath "the rhetoric of racial and cultural retrieval" (Nzenza 216). In particular, Florence Stratton has urged female African authors to refute, or refuse, Achebe's gendered framework. Her essay "How Could Things Fall Apart For Whom They Were Not Together?" points to the systematic exclusion of women from all non- domestic aspects of community power in the novel. Following Stratton, the argument that Achebe's gendered depiction of Ibo life is historically 'accurate' can be challenged on the basis that he "could have done more to question those relations" (Booker 73). Although Traoré has called such readings "culturally illiterate" (66), drawing attention to the manner in which the imposed values of Western feminism might be a form, albeit well-intentioned, of cultural imperialism, it is clear that the "reactionary masculinity" (Hogan 125) embodied by Okonkwo (driven to despise everything his father loved, he rejects 'effeminate' gentleness along with laziness) is also rife in his wider society. As Traoré concedes, Okonkwo's suicide is in many ways "a direct result of the ...attempt to displace the *Nneka* principle in his private and public life" (50), and it is notable that, while Achebe is consciously concerned with enforcing a sense of the need for societal equilibrium, the overriding proverbial wisdom that 'mother is supreme' never translates from the symbolic to the level of literal or personal experience. Okonkwo's mother remains nameless in the text, alluded to only in reference to the silliness of her stories (TF 66). Even the hospitality of his motherland Mbanta is experienced as a form of punishment for a lesser, that is, female, crime.

Champion wrestler Okonkwo's misogynist tendencies are certainly heightened beyond the cultural norm, with his insistence upon the retelling and reenactment of "masculine stories of violence and bloodshed" (TF 47) contrasted to the compassionate Nwoye's respect, even preference, for women's wisdom. Similarly, Okonkwo's participation in the killing of adopted son Ikemefuna, stemming from his own (feminine) fear of "failure and weakness" (12), is condemned as unnecessary and undesirable by Obierika. However, the general economy of Umuofia also rests on gendered distinctions. Not only was "Yam, the king of crops...a man's crop" (21), but yam ownership was a greater status symbol than marriage: Okoye is lauded as having "a large barn full of yams" and "three wives" (6), in that order. *Agbala*, the word for "woman," is "also used of a man who has taken no title" (TF 'Glossary'): both, then, are implicitly insulting. Women, as property, are subjected to violence, and it is significant that the earth goddess Ani does not punish Okonkwo for the act of beating Ojiugo (his anger at her having gone to plait her hair instead of cooking was, the narrator decrees, "justifiable" (25)), but merely for doing so during the Week of Peace. The narrative "backs away" (Stratton 28) from fertile gaps or spaces in which these inequalities might be questioned, as do the female characters. The Chielo-Ezinma-Ekwefi encounter might be read as a woman-centered paradigm of resistance: three strong females enacting powerful roles priestess, child, courageous mother in a situation where Okonkwo's "machete, the symbol of his male aggression, is of no use at all" (Davies 247). Intriguingly, the priestess interrupts Ezinma just as she is on the cusp of relating how Tortoise and Cat "went to wrestle against Yams" (88), that dominant male symbol, with the unresolved ending of the fable a potential site of disruption. Such possibilities, however, are subsumed within the prevailing phallocentric story. The feisty Ezinma, who might have figured more in Achebe's narrative, as in Okonkwo's affections, had she been a boy, is, after all, merely one of those infantilised women who, instinctively, "took to their heels" (79) when the (male) egwugwu appeared, fleeing submissively from the centre of political and religious authority. Tellingly, although Achebe does not romanticise Ibo life, the implied male narrator fails to question the injustice suffered by women, and for the most part, the female victims endure with minimal complaint, even silence. Stratton warns that, published at a time when political power was being transferred from the colonial regime to a "Nigerian male elite" (27), such fictional representations risk legitimating the exclusion of women from contemporary public affairs. Indeed, just as the first "nationalist" authors "had to rewrite and reinvent a *presence* that colonialist discourse, in its arrogance, imposture, and triumphalism, had theorized as absence", so too have female writers been motivated to recover the "submerged female traditions" of artistic expression in order to rise above the seemingly "inevitable, natural *sexism*" (Jeyifo 190, 183) often perpetuated by male writers. In taking the pen into their own hands, female writers are becoming an increasingly powerful force, asserting rightful demands for respect, recognition and participation in the formation of a range of positive postcolonial futures.

Challenging the reductive representation of women and advocating improvement in their social and material conditions is a major feminist concern, but, in the 'Third World', women's existence is "strung between traditionalism and modernity in ways that make it extremely difficult for them to attain personal freedoms without severe sacrifices or compromises" (Quayson 103-4), a struggle illustrated to great effect in *Nervous Conditions*. As Mohanty has argued in "Under Western Eyes: Feminist Scholarship and Colonial Discourses" (1994), some feminist writers "discursively colonize" by imagining a composite, singular, "third-world woman" (cited in Quayson 104). This may explain why "the role of 'Africa' in 'post-colonial theory' is different from the role of 'post-colonial theory' in Africa" (McClintock 260): the former often dangerously symbolic, the latter, so far removed from material reality as to be irrelevant, even counterproductive.

Dangarembga's work, the first novel by a black Zimbabwean woman to be published in English (Vizzard 205), is so important to postcolonial understandings (in Africa and in the West) because it displays the vast differences, in aspirations and approaches, both within and between class and generational groupings of Zimbabwean women. Each of the women Tambudzai and her cousin Nyasha, Ma'Shingayi (Tambu's mother) and Maiguru, Lucia, Anne the servant, Tambudzai's grandmother, even the "family patriarch" (NC 142-3) Tete Gladys are aware of the patriarchal incursions upon their lives; but they negotiate very different paths through the complex matrix of "triple" (W.D. Ashcroft 23) colonisation or oppression. These women experience "the poverty of blackness on one side," with the effects of white colonial rule in 1960s Rhodesia, as well as "the weight of womanhood on the other" (NC 16), with ramifications in both traditional and European frames that compound and intensify as they coincide. In addition, they deal with the fraught fusion of emancipatory strategies in a desired "genuine post-colonial feminism" (W.D. Ashcroft 33), rather than merely an Anglo- American or French body of theory transplanted onto the very different actualities of the former colonies. All of the characters, including the men, are linked in the text to nerves, frustration, powerlessness and anxiety, but the confusion resulting from colliding cultural and gender norms is most palpably apparent in the experience of Nyasha, her body providing "testimony" (Suleri 341) to her psychic disruption as she expels that which she cannot digest, or reconcile. The combination of sadza and foreign sweets and biscuits, along with all they represent, is indeed disturbing; but, unlike Tambu, who can eventually "question things and refuse to be brainwashed" (NC 204) by both imported ideals and imposed inferiorities, asserting the independent will to education and change within the overarching "rules of their community's paradigms" (Kalu 153), Nyasha experiences a kind of homelessness, and emptiness, of self and intellect.

Nyasha's socialisation in England may have taught her of her right to stand up for what she believes in (which in turn inspires Tambudzai to look beyond the edges of what she knows), but, alienated from Shona language and norms, she is left without a firm belief for which to fight, only a paralysing sense of the looming problems. Shredding the one-sided history books "between her teeth" (NC 201), Nyasha feels "trapped" by the "Englishness" against which Tambudzai's mother has warned, but she is simultaneously constrained by her father's inability to see his family's, and society's, pre-existing and perpetuated problems of gender inequality, "punching him in the eye" after he calls her a "whore" (NC 114-5). As Tambudzai observes, "the victimization" is, in many ways, "universal. It didn't depend on poverty, on lack of education, or on tradition...Men took it everywhere with them", such that, at base, all "conflicts came back to this question of femaleness," and presumed inferiority (NC 115-6).

It has been suggested that Orientalism (and Africanism) are fantasies built upon sexual difference, with the phallocentric discourse of colonialism inscribing the landscape and population of the exotic 'other' as weak, inferior, yielding and feminine (Yegenoglu 11-12). *Nervous Conditions,* without suppressing "an ounce of its legitimate anger at the misogyny of African men" (Sugnet 36), shows clearly the manner in which those men may themselves be the emasculated products, and puppets, of a colonial hierarchy. The title and epigraph point to Sartre's introduction to Fanon's *The Wretched of the Earth,* which asserts that "the status of 'native' is a nervous condition introduced and maintained by the settler among colonized people *with their consent*" (quoted in Booker 191), a kind of psychological subordination. Although Dangarembga's main concern is

91

with "feminizing Fanon's findings on colonial cultural alienation" (Boehmer 228), the male characters are portrayed as having been bewitched by colonialism. Split between loyalty to tradition and the desire to share the perceived material benefits of 'modern' culture, they are led to "accept their own inferiority" (Booker 191), thus cooperating in their subjugation, with both Tambudzai's father and brother suffering "painfully under the evil wizards' spell" (NC 50). Jeremiah, a parody of the 'shiftless native', brandishes an imaginary spear while becoming reliant on the generosity of his Western-educated brother, while Babamukuru, kept "busy" (102) between the demands of life as a surrogate Englishman and traditional obligations to his extended family, is haunted by the sense that, created by the British colonial system to serve its purposes, his power is illusory. At the Sacred Heart Convent school he, like Tambu, is a mere black face, an (inferior, segregated, undifferentiated) "African" (NC 194). Even Mr Matimba, in order to assist Tambu sell maize to fund her schooling, is forced to perform a subservient and compliant role with white people, speaking "in the softest, slipperiest voice I had ever heard him use" (27). These curtailments and false reshaping of self are spiritually stunting, even fatal: Tambu's brother Nhamo dies, if indirectly, because of his attempt to transcend altogether the 'dirty', cumbersome realities of African communal life. While Tambu herself acknowledges, and for a time even succumbs to, the seductions of a clean, clear-cut white world, Dangarembga ingeniously demonstrates that what colonial discourse defines as 'African' is often really "the debased form of indigenous ways *after* colonialism has disrupted them" (Sugnet 44). The apparently straightforward symbolism of hygiene at first seems clearly arranged in favour of English customs, but Tambu soon reverses her conviction that "the further we left the old ways behind the closer we came to progress" (NC 147). There may be "reproductive odors", children with "upset bowels" and strong "aromas of productive labour" (1) on the slow Umtali bus, but the sparkling white porcelain of Maiguru's bathroom actually suppresses normal bodily functions (making Tambu's menstrual blood seem "nasty and nauseating" (95)), and masks the pathological. The filthiness of the pit toilet is as much a symptom of colonial disease as is Nyasha's vomit: in the "early days" before Tambu's mother 'lost' her children to a new way of life, along with her pride and reason for living, the latrine "had never smelt and its pink plaster walls had remained a healthy pink" (NC 123). Much as an 'unadapted' English vocabulary might be inadequate to convey African realities, so too do housing structures derived from English circumstances have difficulty coping with the African "dust" (NC 71) which, creeping pervasively in, widens existing class and gender inequalities. Although Maiguru has been educated overseas like her husband, her wages are subsumed within his; her point of view goes largely unacknowledged; and, although she breaks free of her baby- talk to leave his reign for a few days, she ultimately returns to serve at table, and maintain, with the help of servant Anne, the deceptively shiny surfaces of their existence, scrubbing at doubts with an ammonia cleaner which was "efficient but chapped your hands much more roughly than ash dissolved in water from Nyamarira ever did" (NC 67).

It has been suggested that Dangarembga sets the novel "back in history in order to blame the colonizers, rather than Mugabe's government, for the plight of women in Zimbabwe" (Sugnet 46), but it is evident that, in writing about "the things that move" (Veit-Wild 29), affect, enrage and inspire women, traditional African patriarchy does not escape unscathed. Dangarembga has spoken of the need to stop subsuming women's issues, which have not yet received "proper attention or the right kind of analysis", within the "national question" (quoted in Osei-Nyame, Jnr 55), and *Nervous Conditions* demonstrates the complicity between colonialism and patriarchy, with pre-colonial forms of oppression merely transplanted onto and exacerbated by Western culture. The narrative achieves a "defamiliarization" (Skinner 116) of gender norms by showing them through 8-year-old Tambu's eye to be (like the concept of racial inferiority) mere cultural constructs. The preferential treatments of sons, and the gendered division of housework, labour and authority in traditional society, are magnified in the context of colonial education: the male role as family breadwinner makes Nhamo the 'natural' choice for further schooling,

increasing his privileges exponentially. Tambu's "callousness" to his death (which is also her window of opportunity) is necessary if she is to "escape" the patterns of "entrapment" (NC 1) she sees around her. Convinced of her own worth, Tambu sees the "injustice" (12) of her mother's acquiescence to learning, "the earlier the better," what "sacrifices" (16) will be necessary. The text enters fully into the "woman-centered spaces" (Aegerter 231) the cooking and sleeping areas as well as the mental and emotional terrain mapped therein providing detailed insights denied to the reader in Achebe's male- centered work. As a result, it becomes clear that modes of female resistance from within a tradition-based contemporary African culture are possible. In an echo back to the village elders' adjudication of Mgbafo's marital dispute in *Things Fall Apart* (77-83), where women are excluded simultaneously from proceedings and from readerly view, the perspective of "we, the women and children" becomes the focus in *Nervous Conditions,* making way for the expression of an attitude of "quite violent...opposition to the system" (NC 137) while the *dare* or male meeting regarding Lucia's sexual transgression is conducted. Determining that "she should be there to defend herself " (137), Lucia storms into the house, eyes glittering, and, tweaking Takesure by the ears, demands some "sense" and honesty. Tambu is later unsure whether the "patriarchy" shared her (disrespectful) "laughter" (144), and is herself racked with physical reaction to the wedding which makes a mockery of her parents' existence, as of her own, but the spirit of the moment resonates throughout the work, and beyond the last page.

Just as Tambu questions the success of Nyasha's "rebellion" (NC 1), the reader may fear that the freedom she claims for herself and Lucia is illusory. Notably, Lucia's declaration that Grade One has made her mind "think more efficiently" (160) is overshadowed by both the colonial ideologies undeniably inherent in the pre-independence syllabus, and the necessity of her "grovelling" to (200) (or, "like a man herself " (171), skilfully manipulating) Babamukuru for assistance. However, Tambu manages to retain positive contact with the spiritual life of the African landscape and her body, immersing herself in "the old deep places" (4) as sources of strength and orientation (rather than succumbing to a reductive identification of the singular subject position, unthinking 'woman', with land and the national identity, able to be raped and lost forever). So too there is a sense that she might be able to break down the "Englishness" (203) to manageable pieces, choosing to consume (rather than be consumed by) some aspects, and rejecting or protesting against others. The young Tambu, fearing that it was "unwise to think too deeply" (39) about sexism lest dissatisfaction "interfere with the business of living", soon learns that to "bury" (50) thoughts and desires for self-fulfilment is to enact a stifling live burial (much as the burial of the voices of female characters in other texts might have contributed to the social and political stasis of their female readers). To truly know "myself," Tambu must speak the "knotted" complex issues that characterise her experience of being African, and being female. Although, like her education at the mission and boarding schools, her self-authorship involves the use of the colonial language, her decision is ultimately an empowering one, and she achieves the authoritative status of "interpreter" (Uwakweh 78), rather than the paraphrased or unheard interpreted subject of knowledge. Dangarembga, like other postcolonial women writers, in her "double…perspective of ethnicity and gender" turns "absence into presence" (Begum 27) by giving voice to a multiplicity of previously silenced or marginalised female viewpoints. While there will always be "another volume" (NC 204) to be filled, and new or altered perspectives from which to write back, this text alone has made important inroads into breaking free of the reductive and stereotypical presentation of African women in literature, thus inspiring positive changes in life.

Appiah has stated that "postcoloniality is the condition…of a relatively small, Western-style, Western-trained, group of writers and thinkers" who have "invented" (149) an Africa for their own use. Such a view might prove as disabling as the notion that 'the subaltern cannot speak', or that self-expression in the once 'colonial' language, English, undermines authenticity: put together, not only would postcolonial writers by definition not be able to communicate but, even if they could, the rest of the world would be too self-absorbed to hear them. Rather, as Darby refreshingly suggests, we may need to alter our mode of approach, so that, instead of becoming caught up in the self-referential requirements of an "often resistant body of theory", we should give much more weight to the "problems", and authors, of the so-called 'Third World': in this respect, "Achebe is a better guide than either Derrida or Foucault" (17).Social responsibility, as well as forming the self-professed motivation of the creative work of authors such as Achebe and Dangarembga, "must be the basis of any theorizing on postcolonial literature" (Katrak 157), necessitating a "good-faith effort" to cultivate "readerly tact" (Linton 29, 43) and responsiveness as non-African readers respectfully approach and seek to understand (but not assimilate to their own Eurocentric perspective) different African "ways of knowing" (Kalu xv). *Things Fall Apart* and *Nervous Conditions*, in dialogue with each other and with texts from the Western 'canon' such as that purveyor of Africanist myths, Conrad's *Heart of Darkness,* provide a positive "way forward" (Dodgson 101) in both the literary and socio-cultural- political domains, encouraging readers to approach the multiplicity of voices they contain in light of the knowledge that, as Achebe has remarked, postcolonial "travellers with closed minds can tell us little except about themselves" (An Image of Africa" 791).

Chapter Six

Identity in a Postcolonial Void

L. Nesbitt

IN the last half of the twentieth century many postcolonial cultures have found themselves out of balance. During colonization the people lived a kind of non-existence, a living void; their identities had been stolen. To establish dominion, the colonial power eradicated previous religions, educational structures, and languages. Although the indigenous person adopted a Western identity through the colonizer, it was an illusion, empty of meaning, because the native culture, in all its complexity, was not recognized by the colonizer. Essentially the people became impostors of themselves. Their personal and cultural history had been destroyed as one of the implications of colonial rule. Since the complex identity of the native was not acknowledged, the native essentially never existed as a unique individual in the colonizer's eyes.

The identity inflicted on the indigenous person was a meaningless stereotype masking the true identity that had become void. This vacancy will be explored from the context of abuse of power. This void is the denial of identity and a life with no meaning; the mask of colonial identity covering the void is an illusion. Taking off the mask in the postcolonial world does not necessarily reveal a full individual; the colonial

98

erasure of cultural and personal identity appears to be permanent.

The enduring exploitation of formerly colonised nations has been defined using the term Neo-colonialism. The term implies a nation with a continued reliance upon the former imperial power and the West in general, but more specifically neo-colonialism also implies a persistent state of confusion of selfhood for the individual and for the whole nation. We spend our lives constructing unique personal traits and individually recognizable selves created from different sources. In the globalisation of today's society, the notion of identity is becoming increasingly complex, especially with an added complication of post-colonization. Many individuals do not communicate in their indigenous language, were not schooled using textbooks reflecting their particular social and cultural situations, or had Western instructors; even their religions did not reflect their own indigenous religious history. The definition of one's self has become multi-layered and essentially fractured.

The departure of the colonizing power forced the postcolonial world out of balance placing the formerly colonized nations into a new and continued version of dependence upon the West. M.G. Vassanji's novel, *The In-Between World of Vikram Lall*, covering fifty years of Kenyan history, focuses on neocolonial imbalance and the elaborate postcolonial reappraisal of cultures. In the beginning of the text, the Kenyan people are on the lowest rung of the social ladder with whites and Indians in power. In 1965 after Kenya assumed political independence and Jomo Kenyatta became president of the new nation, an elaborate repositioning of the classes occurred. This tumultuous period contributed to a chaos that fed lawless activities, realigning individuals in

Western nations with Kenyan politicians and private citizens in the extortion that harmed the Kenyan people yet again.

Vassanji's elaborate novel depicts an international racketeering allowing some individuals like the protagonist, Vik, to get very rich. The novel begins with a confession:

> My name is Vikram Lall. I have the distinction of having been numbered one of Africa's most corrupt men, a cheat of monstrous and reptilian cunning. To me has been attributed the emptying of a large part of my troubled country's treasury in recent years. I head my country's List of Shame. (Vassanji 3)

Through his employer Vik is involved with an illegal scheme in which private individuals essentially operate their own bank with no government restrictions, providing the government no financial benefit. Kenya is a "country of ten millionaires and ten million paupers" (Vassanji 259). Vik is in the middle of a handful of Kenyans who profit enormously from European and American fraud.

Using Vik's childhood friend, Njoroge, as a symbol of the Kenyan people and their resistance movement, we can conclude that Vik's illegal activities essentially contribute to Njoroge's death. In the beginning of the novel, Njoroge sympathizes with the Mau Mau, refers to Jomo Kenyatta as the Black Moses, and takes Vik to a meeting of "former freedom fighters Mau Mau, as they used to be called" (Vassanji 153). Later in the novel, Njoroge realizes that Jomo Kenyatta, the man he believed would lead the Kenyans to a better future, had become corrupt and the Mau Mau have been betrayed. Njoroge is killed by a political rival of Kariuki, the honest man he hopes will become president, who is also the rival of Jomo Kenyatta, the man Vik is enabling to profit from the illegal scam. This complicated entanglement leading to Vik's enormous profits essentially links Vik's actions to Njoroge's murder. At the end of the novel Vik's realization of the ramifications of his scam leads to his suicide.

Kenya is out of balance; its people suffer because of a corrupt government with corrupt politicians and self-serving, greedy men and women. Kenya is also still economically dependent upon the West. Vik is the middle-man in a lucrative hustle that brings American dollars into the country so that Jomo Kenyatta's government will stay in power. Paul Nderi, Kenya's Minister of Transport and Vik's boss, tells Vik:

> These are donations to our party from well-wishers abroad. ...Honest-to-God donations from private individuals. I would like you to find your Indian contacts and have them change this money and stash it; like in a bank. . . . And when our different constituencies need money for their operations, they will be paid by those Indians. (Vassanji 257)

Although there is no direct implication by Nderi of any Western nation, it is clear that corruption has spread throughout all cultures in Kenya and throughout the West. Even though Nderi is not a trustworthy character, the reader can believe that the two men with whom Vik exchanges money-stacked suitcases are American citizens. While it is possible that millions of dollars are given by private American citizens who are concerned about the possibility of a "great danger from the communists" (Vassanji 256); it is also highly unlikely that one individual would have access to so much cash and would be altruistically concerned solely with the Kenyan government. Therefore, this draining of Kenya's wealth is an example of neo-colonialism, an enduring exploitation of a formerly colonised nation creating a continued reliance upon the West, implicating the American government. The people who suffer the most grievously are the majority of the Kenyan people. As a symbol of those people, Njoroge is the only true innocent.

Throughout the essay "On National Culture," Frantz Fanon argues that a native writer assists in the process of cultural and personal re- identification by acting as a communicator of the national struggle to the people. It is the writer's task and unique ability to use literature to describe the illusion, the void, and thereafter, the imbalance created. He can evoke the identification process from the culture of which he writes. Fanon clarifies this potential in his interpretation of a poem by Keita Fodeba: "The understanding of the poem is not merely an intellectual advance, but a political advance. There is not a single colonized person who will not perceive the message that this poem holds" (Fanon 231). By using his own heart for exploration, the native author communicates the struggle to the people, and thereby helps the people begin to define a new voice. In removing his own colonial mask of illusion, the writer assists each individual in their own private struggle to remove the illusory mask.

On the one hand Fanon implies that there is an old identity in which the indigenous person can be re-attired. However, he also acknowledges that the old identity is extinct. Relying on the security of a past identity is problematic:

> The artist who has decided to illustrate the truths of the nation turns paradoxically toward the past and away from actual events. What he ultimately intends to embrace are in fact the castoffs of thought, its shells and corpses, a knowledge which has been stabilized once and for all. But the native intellectual who wishes to create an authentic work of art must realize that the truths of a nation are in the first place its realities. He must go on until he has found the

seething pot out of which the learning of the future will emerge. (Fanon 225)

If the artist puts on a destroyed mask, it reinforces the abstraction of stereotype and the idea that the ghost of the past is an empty white sheet. Even though Fanon believes it is possible to re-wear that stereotype, he also believes it is worthless and that no future exists by wearing the empty mask. It is the chaotic present that holds the essence of the future. Moreover, it is only the first of three stages that the native intellectual will progress through before he becomes "an awakener of the people" (Fanon 223). While the present may contain elements of the past, for example language, even the native language itself is in the process of transformation; and it is that transformation that is the key to progress.

Fanon's argument for a people's revolution focuses on Algeria and the still present French colonialist power (1963); but the reasoning behind his argument can be generally applied to many, if not all states. His notions are relevant to a postcolonial world and the issue of neo- colonialism. The native intellectual must analyze and communicate the struggle to the people in a language they will understand; this is empowering to the most vulnerable class, those without money and power, the majority of the population.

Ngugi wa Thiong'o, whose first novels were written in English, the colonizer's language, has long chosen to write in his native Gikuyu rather than English. Historically the Gikuyu people are an oral culture. According to Ngugi, although the Gikuyu may not have the money to buy his books, they discuss his ideas in community gatherings. By his choice of language, Ngugi accepts and acknowledges the importance of his role as communicator and facilitator these discussions:

It was easy for people to write in the language of their colonization because it was the language of their conceptualization, the language of education, the language in which they attempted to intellectually grasp the world around them. I believe that the language issue is a very important key to the decolonization process. What is really happening now is that African thought is imprisoned in foreign languages. (*Interviews* 30)

In other words, African identity has been stolen. When the colonisers replaced the Gikuyu language and when the education system was translated into a Western one, it weakened Gikuyu identity. When the writer communicates to the people in Gikuyu, he is making a conscious decision to communicate to the majority of the people in a language they can trust and understand. Potentially there are unique thoughts within the Gikuyu language that can only be expressed with that language. Paradoxically, language is a portion of the old identity, but it is also a tool which can transform and be manipulated to shape the present, becoming an essential part of the new identity. Moreover, the development of a new language creates new identity; it does not resurrect an old one. Accordingly, since the texts chosen for this paper are written in English, perhaps there might be something missing or lacking. However, what can be gained from the cultural variety of texts is the notion that the postcolonial void ignores international boundaries.

The colonising agents of education, religion, and language erase individuality and contribute to instability in the world in each of the following texts. Each text depicts a different stage of colonial power: the imposition of rule, the initial occurrences of strikes against colonial authority, and the effects of colonization. In the first text, several things fall apart with the imposition of colonial rule: a man's life; his tribe; and Nigeria, his country. Achebe begins *Things Fall Apart* by quoting the first four lines of 'The Second Coming' by W.B. Yeats:

> Turning and turning in the widening gyre The falcon cannot hear the falconer; Things fall apart; the centre cannot hold; Mere anarchy is loosed upon the world.

Yeats's notion that humans have created a dark and foreboding future with no connection between their own humanity and spirituality is implicit and explicit in Achebe's novel. There is a loss of common purpose, instability, and great unrest in a world spinning out of control.

The novel is replete with symbolism emphasizing these notions. For example several of Achebe's characters function as symbols. While Okonkwo, the protagonist, is a complex character, he also symbolizes traditional Igbo society; he is defined by his culture, clan, and his rigid role in that clan. He is also a flawed character with some of his destruction being self-inflicted. For example even though he is warned not to participate in the killing of his surrogate son, he fears "being thought weak" and so strikes the fatal blow (Achebe 43). This blow destroys his family since it drives his son to the colonizer's religion where he is given a new self-identity, "Isaac" (Achebe 129). On the one hand Okonkwo's resolute behaviour kills him and contributes to the fracturing of his tribe; however, his daughter, Ezinma, symbolizes the future of the clan when she crawls into the cave and womb-like safety of Africa, transported on the back of the oracle, Chielo.

Religion is clearly represented as a colonising agent; the missionaries reject the authenticity of indigenous beliefs and thereby contribute to the colonising process by stripping away the already present and functioning religion and converting to Western education. Missionaries are responsible for sending Okonkwo's son to a British school where he is renamed. Therefore, Okonkwo's determined nature is only a part of the destructive force: "From the very beginning religion and education went hand in hand" in the colonization of Nigeria (Achebe 128). The benevolence of both education and religion reduce Okonkwo and his whole clan to "not a whole chapter but a reasonable paragraph" in the colonial text: "The Pacification of the Primitive Tribes of the Lower Niger" (Achebe147-8). Therefore, missionaries contribute to the death of the clan since they are responsible for the loss of their next generation: "Nwoye, who was now called Isaac, [is sent] to the new training college for teachers" (Achebe 129).

The dichotomy is that the Igbo will let the white people stay and worship their own gods: "It is good that a man should worship the gods and the spirits of his fathers. Go back to your house so that you may not be hurt. Our anger is great but we have held it down so that we can talk to you" (Achebe 134). The Igbo are a very peaceful culture and will accept a Western god; but, their welcoming nature contributes to the destruction of their clan, since Western religion does not recognize any other gods. The distinctiveness of the Igbo culture is eradicated through religion and education:

> Our own brothers who have taken up his religion also say that our customs are bad. How do you think we can fight when our own brothers have turned against us? The white man is very clever. He came quietly and peaceably with his religion. We were amused at his foolishness and allowed him to stay. Now he has won our brothers, and our clan can no longer act like one. He has put a knife on the things that held us together and we have fallen apart. (Achebe 124-5)

106

Okonkwo is aware of how some white men have colonized and destroyed another village. He cannot allow other white men to destroy his own village since his own sense of self is represented by traditional Igbo culture; the destruction of his village would imply the destruction of himself. Clearly, for Okonkwo he must kill the white messenger. He then hears members of his tribe questioning his actions. He now understands that his tribe has fallen apart; therefore, he has fallen apart. Okonkwo has no future since there is no future for his tribe. He has lost his identity. Death is his only alternative.

Religion and education as colonizing agents also dominate the text of *Weep Not, Child*, by Ngugi wa Thiong'o. The protagonist, Njoroge, also completely accepts Western education and religion. The novel is a Bildungsroman for Njoroge, an innocent child with a dream to go to an English school and complete faith in "the righteousness of God" (Ngugi 49). Njoroge symbolizes the Gikuyu people. He has a dream of a "bright future" in which he will "have a shirt and shorts for the first time" (Ngugi 3-4). He believes himself to be a saviour or religious leader for the Gikuyu: "His task of comforting people had begun" (Ngugi 95). This notion supports an allusion to Jomo Kenyatta, previously discussed in Vassanji's novel, the leader of the Mau Mau and president of Kenya. The people believed that Jomo would save them and their country. But when Jomo became president, eventually the government became corrupt. Njoroge's dreams are also broken and lost in the illusion of the coloniser: "'The sun will rise tomorrow,' he said triumphantly, looking at her as if he would tell her that he would never lose faith, knowing as he did that God had a secret plan" (Ngugi 106). Njoroge's dream, like the Kenyan people's dream, is shattered at the end of the novel by a corrupt government still economicallydependent upon the West.

This benevolent gift of Western religion and education proves to be an elaborate deception. Njoroge walks through the woods with his teacher, a Gikuyu who has now re-identified himself as Isaka, while "discussing the saving power of Christ" (Ngugi 101). White soldiers stop them and murder Isaka after accusing him of being a terrorist. Then white men take Njoroge from his school and beat him so badly that he falls into a coma. Soldiers torture and castrate Ngotho, his father, who dies from the torture. After so much tragedy, life itself becomes "a big lie" for Njoroge (Ngugi 126). While ironically recalling his lost faith, Njoroge considers his religious belief and Western ideals:

O, God But why did he call on God? God meant little to him now. For Njoroge had now lost faith in all the things he had earlier believed in, like wealth, power, education, religion. Even love, his last hope, had fled from him. (Ngugi 134)

Njoroge realizes that this Western charitable deception would ultimately lead to his pacification. He now understands that as soon as he would have become educated and developed his own voice, any hope of power or wealth would have been taken away: "I know that my tomorrow was an illusion" (Ngugi 132). His identity as defined by Western religion and education and as imposed by colonialism was an empty illusion.

Ngugi chooses a protagonist who symbolizes innocence and total acceptance of colonial conformity. Since Njoroge is a child his life is comparatively easy to disrupt and overwhelm with a new self-identity. He is easy to deceive and once his fragile identity is erased, he has nothing to fall back on. On the other hand, Okonkwo has a more fully formed sense of self and will not accept defeat; but because Okonkwo is a lone voice with no other men from the tribe supporting him, his voice will not be heard. It is clear with all both characters that their loss of self-identity is complete. They are unable to return to any past religion, education or cultural definition of themselves through their clans or alone.

Therefore, the mask of Western identity is an illusion. This idea is clearly supported by the texts: Western education, religion, and language simply do not function for Njoroge, Okonkwo, and Vik. Moreover, once the colonizer has left, the enormity of the remaining void is so overwhelming that each character either contemplates or commits suicide. There is literally nothing left to live for when the illusion and deception of a Western identity is revealed.

Specifically Okonkwo's clan no longer supports him, rather they support the Western intruders; his son no longer practices the indigenous religion and has been given a Christian name; and Okonkwo sees no future since he refuses to accept colonial domination. Okonkwo hangs himself even though suicide "is an abomination. ...[and] his body is evil, and only strangers may touch it" (Achebe 147). However, his clan pays him a final, clarifying tribute: "That man was one of the greatest men in Umuofia. You drove him to kill himself; and now he will be buried like a dog" (Achebe 147). Njoroge also contemplates suicide and sits holding a rope with which he hopes to hang himself at nightfall. He hears an evil voice urging him to "*Go on!*" and kill himself (Ngugi 135). He laughs while contemplating his action. It is futile to attempt to go against the Western colonizers. However, Njoroge does not commit suicide:

His mother was looking for him. For a time he stood irresolute. Then courage failed him. He went towards her, still trembling. And now he again seemed to fear meeting her. He saw the light she was carrying and falteringly went towards it. It was a glowing piece of wood which she carried to light the way. (Ngugi 135)

While carrying a burning candle, his mother brings him back to the clan. The only place Njoroge can establish and create a new identity is with his own people joining their struggle to survive. At the end of *The In-Between World of Vikram Lall*, Vik also sees a glow from a fire. It is surrounding a man who calls to Vik from the bottom of a staircase, attempting to save his life. However, Vik chooses to run away from the glow and kill himself. Ultimately Vik cannot forget his betrayal of his people.

Symbolically the idea of re-weaving and re-creating a connection with one's tribe can be seen in Achebe's novel. Immediately after hearing her mother tell a folk story about a Tortoise falling from the sky and smashing into pieces symbolising the fall of the British, Ezinma, Okonkwo's daughter, is called by the oracle. Chielo specifically calls upon and addresses her prophecy to Ezinma, the symbol of African hope: "Chielo never ceased in her chanting. She greeted her god in a multitude of names the owner of the future, the messenger of earth" (Achebe 75). Ezinma's womanhood is of interest since Okonkwo is "specially fond of Ezinma" (Achebe 32), and in fact, "never stopped regretting that Ezinma was a girl" (Achebe 122). Since Okonkwo represents the past and the traditional values of the clan, he cannot appreciate Ezinma because of her womanhood; but he does appreciate her value. She symbolizes rebirth and the future of the clan. Immediately after Ezinma listens to the allegorical folk tale, she begins a journey to a cave on Chielo's back. As the priestess carries the girl into the night, Ezinma redefines her social identity by submitting to a dangerous ordeal, a liminal phase, prior to reintegrating with her family and clan. The future will be found in the union of native people sharing their struggle, courageous enough to create new religion, language, and educational systems.

A void is left with the disappearance of the colonial power; the economic and political power structure is gone, and each individual is bereft of a definition of himself. Neo-colonialism maintains the relationship with the colonizer rendering the people once again devoid of an identity. The process of community organization is the essential step in the process of re-identification of both the individual and the state. The people's struggle is where the new identity is born:

> We believe that the conscious and organized undertaking by a colonized people to re-establish the sovereignty of that nation constitutes the most complete and obvious cultural manifestation that exists.
>
> . . . The struggle for freedom does not give back to the national culture its former value and shapes; this struggle which aims at a fundamentally different set of relations between men cannot leave intact either the form or the content of the people's culture. After the conflict there is not only the disappearance of colonialism but also the disappearance of the colonized man. (Fanon 245-6)

Fanon's focus is on the genesis of national culture and thereby of the discovery of a separate and unique personality. Nation-building as a process not only emerges when the colonizer is in power, but continues in the postcolonial period and creates the new identity.

Therefore, while the colonial erasure of identity appears a permanent condition, by allowing the re-emerging state and individual to define new selves, the culture will be reborn.

Fanon defines this re-emergence of identity as a people's revolution placing great importance on individuals organizing at the community level and emphasizing the assistance of the native intellectual in the form of a writer and artist. He also places importance on appreciating the individual citizen and the individual state as unique entities, not as oversimplified concepts. Therefore Nigeria and Kenya are not merely anonymous postcolonial states containing indistinctive postcolonial men and women; they are regions with ancient historical backgrounds that contain, in the present, unique human beings who are re-creating their political, cultural, linguistic, and religious identities. Not only must new selves be re-created, but neo-colonial interference based upon economic greed must be eliminated.

Chapter Seven

Trojan Alternatives

C. Ce

Colonisation and Alienation

IT could not have been too obvious to Christopher Columbus (or the unaccredited earlier 'discoverers' of the West Indies before him) that his journeys across the Bahamas late in the fifteenth century would mark the formative stages of modern Caribbean history and culminate in a new landscape mired in conflicts and controversy. Ditto for the Lander brothers whom Europe credits with the discovery of the Niger River, one of nature's bounteous endowments on the African continent which existed and had been known to the natives long before his time. What had led early historians to assert ironically that the Caribbean is merely a geographical expression that lacks a noteworthy history and Africa a land of poverty and disease can be found at the centre of this historical movement of cross racial encounters. It boils down to the history of colonial men who leave their shores searching for fortune —as an African poet would put it— 'in the hearts of distant lands.' (*Moon* 6)

Most of contemporary critical opinion about the West Indies is likewise connected with the colonial attitude toward Africa and endures in the general dilemmas of post colonial

African states that Emerged in the 20 century from crude amalgamations by their founding masters. Colonial intrusions in Africa and other parts of the New World laid the seeds of more sophisticated tribal rivalries and conflicts at so-called independence. For instance, the Assimilation policy of the colonial French government in West Africa left a record of exploitation and dependency syndrome that put Africa's economy perpetually on the receiving end. On the individual plank, French policy at best succeeded in the creation of a hybrid African whose destiny was failure in all political, social and economic fronts; the only redemptive alternative being the rejection of Europe's Trojan gift of civilisation. In a bid to become African Frenchmen the new product of colonial education was made and encouraged to turn his back on his traditional values. This alienated attitude of self derision became part of the enduring notions of the westernised African. On the continental level African states after the imperial adventure became mere geographical curvatures that satisfied the predatory instincts of the west whose only morality had always been the force of the cudgel and their control of the instruments of propaganda and thought.

Of significance in this study is the West Indian (VS Naipaul) and African (Mongo Beti) novelists' response to the consequences of the colonial encounter through the memories of their characters and the development of the post colonial dialogue in the minds and thoughts of individuals who are representatives of particular cultural and historical stages of growth and transformation. The writer's vision of history and the impact of his assessment, if borne from a continuing tradition of self analysis is the subject of this critical assessment bearing in mind the power of the creative medium of literature in developing and refashioning a credible response of people to history and experience.

The nineteenth- and twentieth-century Africa saw British and French interests formed around oppositions that forever impacted negatively on the continent's political development. Britain on her part continued with her Divide-and-Rule policy to wreak havoc in the culturally diverse West African polities even after independence. Symptoms of exploitation and retardation of the colonies abound throughout the African region. In French West Africa the Assimilation policy had tried unsuccessfully to make French citizens of educated Africans. This idea of re-making the native was the height of cultural imperialism. The colonial imperative of producing Frenchmen out of black men presupposed that the native cultures were of an aberrant tradition as against the assumed superiority of the colonial power which by the way is the power of brigandage and continued exploitation and impoverishment of the weaker. So in practice these products of the colonialist experiment were neither Frenchmen nor eventually fully Africans. In their reassessment of the French heritage some of the foremost writers of Africa's independence generation and products of the colonial experiment such as Mongo Beti, would denounce colonisation and the effects it had on traditional societies (ASC 1.)

Like its African counterpart modern West Indian society must be traced to the circumstances of its discovery and the ensuing exploitation of its human and economic resources. Even some parts of the physical environment itself were imported: domestic animals, cereals, vegetables, fruits and sugar cane brought by the colonists. The mineral and agricultural resources of the area served for personal benefits and for the development of Spain, Portugal, Britain and the Netherlands. For these colonial nations, the lure of gold, sugar and slaves accelerated their greedy forage in these territories.

Western powers fought to obtain a considerable share of Caribbean wealth and this gave rise naturally to piracy, double-dealings and lack of cohesion among them (King 6-7). Consequently, colonial rivalries, post colonial isolationism and the endemic sense of provincialism all proved difficult to eradicate even in 20 century Caribbean mentality. The cane plantation which was the basis for the colonial institution and slavery was to have a demeaning influence on the Caribbean psyche for decades.

Cultural diversity in the Caribbean islands (Asian immigration between 1838 and 1934 alone saw the introduction of about ½ million indentured Indian labourers) further helped to rob the inhabitants of a sense of unity and emphasised their lack of control over their lives (*Calcutta* 78). Since the inhabitants of the Caribbean either migrated or were forcibly transferred there, excepting the indigenous Indian population which nevertheless, was finally exterminated, the West Indies became an artificially created society. East Indians were from the beginning rated at the bottom of the social ladder. Being the last of immigrant farmers, they were usually impoverished; they did not speak English, had no western education and brought their native culture and religions with them (100). This led to aggravated racial, linguistic and cultural dichotomies. The Caribbean became a deterministic society that predicated social status upon colour pigmentation and where people were divided into exclusive colour compartments. This situation intensified the psychosis nurtured by a sense of racial and cultural void. Various stereotypes calcified into solid prisms through which the different races observed themselves, a feature of post colonial African nationalities that often degenerated into protracted and rancorous civil wars in the continent.

116

The history of the Caribbean and modern African states has so far been consistent as a record of displaced values. From this emotional, cultural, spiritual, environmental, social and economic displacement arose psychological traumas, symptoms of alienation, rootlessness and an endemic colonial mentality. In this recall of memory Derek Walcot captures the acute sense of loss of the inhabitants in two cryptic lines:

We left
Somewhere a life we never found
(King, 123)

This tragic reality common to both French and English speaking West Indian products justifies Aime Cesaire's question: "Being such as we are can that rush of virility, the conquering knee of victory, the clouded fertility of that plain which is the future ever be ours?" (*Writing* 75).

West Indian writers hold different memories of their history. George Lamming perceives the recognition and identification of a writer to be predicated on the sensibilities which the writer articulates. "A Negro writer," he observes "is a writer who encounters himself in a category called Negro ...(and who) carries this definition like a limb. It travels with him as a necessary guide for the Other's regard..."(77) Experience thus reinforced in memory is, by extension, to the Caribbean writer the gift of identity. Derek Walcot's idea of a "fusion of races," which "involves a mixture of guilty pasts, but from (which) mixture rebirth is possible" (122) suggests that the void poses a challenge to the West Indians to provide and create a positive alternative. The West Indian becomes "a new Adam, a Robinson Crusoe making his own civilization from various cultural roots, but creating something new, unique to the region." (122).

Walcott's sense of optimism hints at the possibility of re-creation, and reordering of memory through which a new consciousness must emerge in the 'new West Indian'. On the contrary, V. S. Naipaul presumes the existence of an overriding Caribbean void where interaction is built upon a cycle of brutality, lack of achievement and mediocrity. In this conundrum individual talents are crippled. All through his writings, Naipaul's inclination for self-contempt would interpret the West Indian historical process as definite, irrevocable and probably irremediable, an attitude comparable in parochialism to that of Trevor Roper who would declare to his Oxford students in the beginning of the twentieth century that Africa had no history. Says V. S. Naipaul in *The Middle Passage:*

> The history of the islands can never be satisfactorily told. Brutality is not the only difficulty. History is built around achievement and creation and nothing was ever created in the West Indies. (29)

This assumption generally provides the basis of appreciating the Naipaulian memory of fragmented and thwarted mediocrity which we find in his characterisation of West Indians in writings such as *The Mystic Masseur* (1957), *Miguel Street* (1959), *A House for Mr Biswas* (1961), *An Area of Darkness* (1964), *The Loss of Eldorado* (1965) and *The Mimic Men* (1967). Naipaul's later novels *In a Free State* (1971), *The Overcrowded Barracoon* (1972), *Guerrillas* (1975), and *A Bend in the River* 1979) are seen to concern with 'the lives of the poverty-stricken Third World, but like *The Middle Passage* are riddled with similar frustration and despair at the possibility of any liberal, radical or nationalist slogans improving the conditions that have caused such hardships in any way' (106). Naipaul himself had often touted himself as not obligated to the Caribbean; not even to his Indian ancestry. He believes West Indian writers have failed in the need for a writer to tell his citizens 'who he is and where he stands.' He does not count himself as among those writers who he claims 'have so far only reflected and flattered the prejudices of their race and colour.' (Passage 68)

Biswas as Paradigm

A House for Mr Biswas projects through the Indian Caribbean consciousness a labyrinth of human interactions in a tangent of perpetual and consistent mockery. As a deeply satirical hero through whom the satirist seeks to ridicule his victims in such a way as to magnify their posturing, Biswas truly emerges if not with very little sympathy but in a clearly ludicrous light for the West Indian man or woman who seeks to triumph over his or her environment. Naipaul concentrates on the struggle between the individual will or desire for a separate identity and the compelling will of the milieu, its anonymity of stifling corporate identity. In *Biswas* the West Indies takes the form of a spiritual desert in which major attempts at creativity and progress are meaningless. Socialization within this milieu involves forcing people to insignificance and robbing them of their freewill. *Biswas* might well be a metaphor of the existentialist journey through life as well as a symbol of the fatalistic Indian philosophy. Therefore Mr. Biswas's relentless fight to possess his own house and steer clear of the grip of the Tulsi's household is seen to parallel man's need to develop a way of life which is uniquely his.

Why Naipaul investigates this making of a new culture in a dominant feature of characters that are failures by their basic inability to express and realise their full creative potential is highly indicative of the colonial retardation with which the writer's environment seems to be afflicted, and which in Naipaulian formula reads: "Ought oughts are ought, ought twos are ought." (*Biswas* 44) Mr. Biswas, who always had a tendency 'to be different' as an individual, is not helped in any way to consummate his individuality or personal identity. From birth, he has had six fingers due to malnutrition; he is fated to have an unlucky sneeze; he is warned never to go near water etc. These inclinations towards being different are consistently shown not to derive from any laudable qualities. Physically, our hero cuts an unimposing figure with his baggy threadbare clothes, distended stomach and soft flabby body. He is acutely aware of his lack of physical endowment and attempts to pre-empt the ridicule of other people by poking fun at himself, a Naipaulian trait evident in all his oeuvres. Mr. Biswas is not sufficiently secure psychologically to survive without a support and identity offered by a family group, yet he constantly rebels against the Tulsi household. When asked to give up painting (which he never excels at) for driving, his reply is "Give up painting? And my independence? No, boy. My motto is: Paddle your own canoe." (107) Freedom comes only from momentary glimpses from the Tulsi's at the deserted shop in the chase, and in the Barracks of Green Vale. But this glimpse is short-lived and based on the illusion of physical freedom which is gained at the confines of Tulsi property.

As a hero Mr. Biswas is never truly free of the Tulsis and whenever he seeks his freedom has to be bailed by members of the Tulsi clan, thus intensifying his subservience and sense of gratitude to them. This is the condition of post colonial states perpetually tied to the apron strings of the colonial overlords under an economy that is dictated by the west for their own entire betterment at the expense of the weaker nations. Until the time he buys his own house, Mr. Biswas is fundamentally lacking in resolve and resorts to making futile expressions of revolt like giving members of the Tulsi family a derogatory name or trying to lose himself in a world of fantasy by writing short stories. On the contrary Mrs Tulsi typifies the slave driver. She resorts to all sorts of emotional blackmail to get her household not to rebel against her dictatorship. She is representative of the slave past of the West Indians and also the post colonial present of West Indian nations.

The omniscient narrative point of view adopted in this novel affords Naipaul to explore the life of each character and present the events to us as they happen. As the all-knowing narrator, the novelist gives us the privilege of sharing the innermost secrets of the characters in different circumstances. Thus the satirical weapon cuts through even the individual characters' foibles and idiosyncrasies, making them the victim at each point of the novel.

The language of this Caribbean novel is creolised. Naipaul's language is characterised by the decadence of the milieu he articulates because of his belief that the West Indies consists of races that have been uprooted from their original society and have not produced a new culture to replace what was lost (103). There is the recurrence of images of destruction and disintegration like 'empty house(s)', 'chaotic dining room(s)', 'offending brick wall(s)' 'sinking floor(s)' amidst the squalor of disintegration all serving to reemphasise futility and hopelessness as far as Naipaul's bleak and befuddled memory of the Caribbean goes.

Naipaul is satirical of the Indian in a New World adhering to customs of the homeland in their bid to establish what ought to be a genuine connection to roots. Hanuman House showcases a crumbling Hindu culture and religion with its tight hierarchical structure leaders, servants, a rigid schedule of prescribed tasks, a scheme of appropriate attitude and a fossilised religious ritual which must be strenuously followed. It is also indicative of the slave society and colonial set up with Mrs. Tulsi as the slave master who being a woman requires the aid of a man, Seth, to validate her authority. These two people need to be worshipped by the subordinates who are also required to help rebuild the crumbling Hanuman Empire. Mrs. Tulsi herself exploits the poverty and helplessness of the Tulsi daughters and husbands. Every husband is carefully selected to ensure that he must conform or, otherwise, be brow-beaten, to the life of the Tulsi's. He must also be from the right caste and must appear to have willingly joined the Tulsi fold. Mrs. Tulsi, like British, French and American slavedrivers and colonialists, is well versed in the psychology of slavery and she knows that she must constantly reinforce her superior position in the household and make her dependants aware of the 'privileges' of performing little tasks for her. To achieve this, she feigns illness frequently in order to elicit guilt and remorse in those who fail to acknowledge her pre-eminence, especially Mr. Biswas, and also to stimulate the unity of her devotees. The children, raised under her tutelage, are ignorant of their dependency and Mr. Biswas who, although acutely aware of this, only engages in spasmodic bursts of rebellion.

Thus we come to see the Tulsi household as representing the entire West Indian society in so far as it totally discourages individuality. All the Tulsi sisters struggle to conform to expected behaviour patterns even to such ridiculous extents as chastising their children. When Mr. Biswas attempts to break his anonymity by giving his daughter a doll's house for Christmas, his wife resents this mark of distinction and can only neutralise it by destroying the house. This action helps heighten the importance of 'house' within the West Indian milieu. Biswas's final attainment of some form of identity is through his ability to get his own house. On another level, Mr. Biswas's badly built and mortgaged house anticipates the problem of the Hindu in Trinidad and the instability of the nation itself.

Naipaul's Caribbean man must therefore be seen as the homeless man. Owning a house may be the symbol of his rehabilitation, as in the case of Biswas, but it seems a tasking, if not Herculean, process. Ultimately Naipaul's vision is sorely affected by a majority of the underprivileged class whose progress and existence are naturally stifled by the planlessness of the society. Change and progress therefore appear a long way ahead as long as the Caribbean society, like its African counterpart, creates mimic men at best whose politics remains a gamble.

Medza as Metaphor

Mission Terminée (translated *Mission to Kala*) written by Mongo Beti (1957) represents the foiled aspirations and stifled destinies of Africa's twentieth century colonial heritage. Educated like most French speaking West Africans in France, Mongo Beti became one of the foremost writers of Africa's independence generation having started his career as a writer in 1953 with the publication of the short story *Sans Haine et sans Amour*. His first novel *Ville Cruelle* followed a year later in 1954. Both works were published under the assumed name of Eza Boto. Two years later came *Le Pauvre Christ de Bomba* under the pseudonym Mongo Beti. Under this name he built up an impressive œuvre, culminating in 2000 with *Branle-bas en Noir et Blanc*. (ascleiden)

It has been commented that Beti's reputation as a writer was firmly established with *Mission to Kala* which aims to subvert colonial rhetoric in order to convince readers to reject the colonial situation (ascleiden). The protagonist of *Mission to Kala* is the individualistic product of French Assimilation (later Association) policy in West Africa. He typifies the African who by his education and reading of western philosophies emerges first as a symbol of this colonial entrapment.

Jean-Marie Medza may not then be seen as a mediocre like Naipaul's Biswas, but an anti-hero; one who, completely overwhelmed by his posturing, fails to retain a credible racial memory save by the patronising and self-immolating terms of his colonial godfathers. From the beginning Medza imagines he is some benevolent conquistador and intends to model his own mission after some Western adventures. If this was not clear enough he obliges us doggedly with echoes of Defoesque in his narrative intros. Chapter Two is explained as a continuation of our hero's great adventure,

> In which the reader, if he is patient, will make the acquaintance of Kala's inhabitants and learn something of their customs and aspirations …(Mission 21)

'The reader', it is further averred 'will also learn of our hero's adventures among the natives of this strange country…' Such expressions as 'natives', 'strange country', etc. are subtle allusions on the one hand to imperial type megalomania typified in the narratives of the Defoes, the Conrads and Carys, and, on the other hand, the symptom of inherited colonial mentality on the part of emerging "African *haut monde*" (Smyth 72). We continually have to deal with

124

these symptoms in this story and halfway, we are forced to note how Medza's mission ridicules the colonial expedition to 'primitive' Africa's hinterland. To further intensify our bemusement, this deliberate caricature of the adventure narratives of western fiction grows anticlimactic and denies any high expectations of the impact it purports to hold.

The discourse of bringing back the runaway wife of his cousin Niam (the mission in itself is predicated upon a domestic matter) is also rendered artlessly, the dialogue untypical of its traditional background because it is filtered through the sensibility of not only a domestically alienated hero but also through characters whose words and utterances are not credible signposts to their customary situations

.

> A pity your father isn't here, my dear cousin, Niam said. But Bikokolo is here, and agrees with me. Do you understand? It isn't just my personal affair any longer. It's a tribal matter. My wife doesn't belong to me exclusively, if you follow me; she's tribal property...so the present situation affects all of us. (11)

We are left in no doubt as to the inadequacy or paucity of linguistic depth in the language of the characters. The African dialogue is consistently corrupted by their stilted speeches: (rather like a chronicle from a colonial visitor's diary) "As you may know it isn't enough to simply marry a woman in our country; even though he follows the prescribed ceremony out to the letter…" On the other hand Medza's language may be deemed appropriate to his cryptic sociological tabloid:

> The chief had just married another wife his seventh as far as I can remember- and he had been in a fine state of anxiety for weeks. Wondering what day his tribal in-laws would choose to deliver his bride on his doorstep. The tribe in question carefully concealed the

day they had selected. They wanted to give the chief a surprise....(125)

Being a product of both worlds of traditional Africa and France by acculturation, Medza's heroism in the eyes of his kinsmen is a distortion of wide reaching dimensions. This irony of distorted reality serves to highlight the ignorance of both worlds which the hero betrays in his final appraisal of his circumstances and those of his kinsfolk.

...those quintessential caricature of the 'civilised' African...(T)he tragedy which our nation is suffering today is that of a man left to his own devices in a world which does not belong to him, which he has not made and does not understand...(181)

Where our "unreliable witness" (Gakwandi 37) assumes the posture of an academic, as in this case, he merely spews the colonial arrogance on the rather much more intricate problem of transitional African societies. He tells us: "It is the tragedy of a man bereft of any intellectual compass, a man walking blindly through the dark in some hostile city like New York..." This "stereotyped thinking about Africa...functionally related to the defense of imperialist interests" (Drake 12) reminds us of Joyce Cary's *Mister Johnson* or even some twentieth century Oxford historians - such as Roper- who believe the entire landscape of Africa is filled with mere savagery and brutality. Our adolescent delinquent wonders about his country folks:

Who will tell him that he cab only cross Fifth Avenue by the pedestrian crossings, or teach him how to interpret traffic signs? How will he solve the intricacies of a subway map, or know where to change trains? (*Mission* 181)

126

Inadvertently here the protagonist bemoans his own failure to understand, if not be fully absorbed in his twentieth century civilisation. In this light he is as much in an ironical position as the story he purports to tell. Here in the young hero's world view lies the future of the post-independent Africa, a future witnessed today in "the buffoonery of the millennium" ('Bards' 23) that characterises the political leaderships and cultural metamorphoses of many colonial creations like Nigeria and Cameroun. This failure of the colonial experiment both at individual and national levels is obvious from the beginning despite the eternal optimism of its apologias. Thus although Medza had failed college examination, for the local 'genius' this is only a minor setback in the journey. For him there is little awareness of a problematic and crumbling colonial education policy, or, if perhaps there was or if it existed, it was only a passing phase. The hero tells us: "by the way I passed college later, " in an attempt to attenuate such minor hiccups in progress, the colonial progress we see him defending petulantly against the critical observations of Kiritikos, the Greek (*Mission* 3)

Medza's reception as a prodigy of learning among his Kala kith and kin should be seen for the irony it is and not merely an indication of the naivety of his kinsmen as critics have been tempted to perceive. Closely knit communities embrace the success of one member as triumph of the whole in much the same principle as the axiom of a spiritual brotherhood that states "when one individual attains enlightenment, the whole of the human race is lifted up..." (*Master* 19) Personal achievements in traditional society are celebrated much as failure is treated with compassion, unlike the opprobrium which the so-called civilised worlds would visit on their heroes who no longer satisfy their urges for a self sacrificing saviour of their own defections. The point here is in agreeing with the critical opinion that "Africa's problems are much more complex than (even) before the....partitioning" (Logan 217) and cannot be oversimplified in the context of acquired Western civilisation.

Consequently the attempt to weigh the uniqueness of the African experience from an entirely westernised attitude and from a poorly conceived traditional rite of passage places the hero in a paradoxical position. In other words, the joke is on himself and not on those "bushmen in the hinterlands." What would have become his growth in awareness grows jagged by the adoption of an overenthusiastic and often deprecatory attitude to paternity and, in extension, nativity– an attitude which does not ameliorate in the end of his (so-called) coming to maturity.

> My father was a real shyster, come to think of it. It was a living example of the astonishing results that can occur when western hypocrisy and commercial materialism are grafted on to a first rate African intelligence.(*Mission* 166)

In this rift between the generations –of incipient capitalism replacing traditional or communal relations– the accomplishments of the older generation (symbolic in Medza's father) does not meet the admiration of their progeny for the reason not entirely inconsistent with the latter's own isolation from the deeper ancestral communion by choice leaving Medza finally seeking the indulgence of an alien racial memory in the final capitulation to the syndrome of modern societies. The novel's first person narrative technique is appropriate as it serves to endow the major character with a mind of his own, consequently Medza is left alone in a world of his own illusions and any redemptive possibility must come from his own acts and his own terns which unfortunately is not realised even till the end of his adventure. At the story's end, the predictable result is the irremediable sense of exile and hopelessness for a lost son for whom the mere bogey of western civilisation is an avenue to befuddled memory and sense of identity. And if one had earlier imagined his colonial mentors being regaled by this exquisite exotica of an adventure, the self exile of Medza and his cousin becomes an act of spiritual atonement in an African sense.

Conclusion

Both *A House for Mr. Biswas* and *Mission to Kala* may be rated as the *metier* of comedians. However, the obvious strengths of both novels lie in their unmitigated and unabashedly satirical and ironical purpose. For Mongo Beti, the treatment of the symptom of modern alienation in the younger African generation in their psychological transition (actually regression) from a state of presumed knowledge (actually ignorance) to a state of maturity (or confusion) exposes from a satirist's artistic discretion the hollowness of the colonial adventure and the consequent entrapment of post colonial societies. Under the temptation to read *Mission* as a perspective on the uneasy gap between the old and emerging young generations, it must be stated that since the young ones, (typified by Medza and his cousin) are quite at home in their alienation, the hero rather comes out as our modern *"ochonga"*[1]- one who makes very little attempt at communal or introspective conciliation save the self-engrossed indulgence of a layabout. His attempts at mocking his society presents us with a probability that often obtains among Africa's elites in their urban environments.

Heroes like Medza remind us of alienated writers forever constrained in the pyrrhic aplomb from their foreign mentors whose prejudice they have vicariously inherited. Another Man-Friday derives from this adventure: the hero, a colonial contrivance, who only seeks to leave behind a mined future for himself and all progeny. To arrogate to the hero of *Mission to Kala* the status of a conquistador on a 'triumphant return from the Kala mission' with the richest of treasures being a better understanding of himself (Biakolo 101) will be a superficial appraisal of one of Africa's ludicrous literary characters -ditto with an attempt to simulate in the thwarted vision of Naipaul some artistic concern with the all-too-familiar existentialism of human life. Between authors Mongo Beti and VS Naipaul however stands a common inclination for the employment of characters that thrive in ridicule and contempt in the effort to simulate historical and psychological reconstruction of race and memory. There is a notable distinction, however, between the one that comes in a manner of a lampoon which presents a pressing need for social revaluation, and the other which merely enforces the writer's vision of a conundrum in which all creative impulse must revolve in atrophy – a vision which rather than edify his primary Caribbean nativity must nevertheless serve to amuse those other proponents and apologists of a Trojan alternative.

Chapter Eight

Desolate Realities

J. N. Nkengasong

IT is often asserted that African Literature was born in the cradle of adversity as an instrument of protest against colonial exploitation and cultural domination. This was in a bid to enforce African nationalism and to protect African culture from being completely obliterated by the overriding Western cultures. Writers on the continent and in the Diaspora therefore, sought to incorporate indigenous African values in their works to the effect that critics of African descent and some foreign scholars find interest mainly in works which treat such subject matter. This, a priori, is not objectionable. However, the slavish search for norms reflecting rudimentary African life, thought and culture in the varied works of African authors might have serious setbacks, the main one being the disregard for some masterpieces which might not after all lay stress on the desired tastes of indigenous African customs.

The critic of Soyinka, for example, is most often infatuated with the playwright's abstruse incorporation of ritual, myth lore and idiom in his works. This is the tendency with Ulli Beier and Gerald Moore, eminent connoisseurs of Soyinka's creative art, who have so earnestly belaboured such themes in volumes of criticism. It is however questionable, if the supposed rich texture in plays like Soyinka's *A Dance of the Forests* and *The Strong Breed* offer more for thought than some of his "simpler" plays like *The Swamp Dwellers*. The resentment is against Moore's use of the expression "least substantial" to obliterate the latter work. He justifies this with the claim that the play offers "none of the extra devices that Soyinka usually employs to enrich his dramatic texture, ranging from verse and song, to dance, masquerade and pantomime" (16). This is certainly misleading because the quest for works which offer the "extra devices" may lead to the obliteration of works which although do not possess these devices may echo more important universal concerns which *The Swamp Dwellers* does.

From another perspective, the tendency in critical thinking is also always to associate the artistic excellence of a writer with the influence of another major writer before him, obliterating the fact that the human consciousness is a residual of archetypal patterns experienced in different epochs and in different geographical spheres. Good examples of archetypal patterns in literature are found in myths. When approached from Carl Gustav Jung's "collective unconscious myths", Maud Bodkin's, Northrop Frye's and Clyde Kluckhohn's postulations one understands myths to be recurrent patterns of beliefs and spiritual concepts in Literature and human history, dealing with themes, experiences and situations, which cut across cultural and geographical boundaries. Clyde Kluckhohn in particular, in his article "Recurrent Themes in Myths and Mythmaking" is quite explicit about

> certain features of mythology that are apparently universal or that have such wide distribution in space and time that result from recurrent reactions of the human psyche to situations and stimuli of the same general order (46).

When one reads the plays of Samuel Beckett and Wole Soyinka against the background of the presumptions of myth criticism cited above, he is compelled to dismiss arguments by critics like Chinweizu et al that Soyinka is one of those "euromodernists, who have assiduously aped" the modes of the 20 century European writers (163); or of Catherine O. Acholonu who states of the playwright in a more specific manner: "Soyinka's themes are echoes of those of Samuel Beckett. His characters are gripped by the same hopelessness in which Beckett's characters find themselves" (15). The fundamental logic applied by Chinweizu and Acholonu in assessing the works of Beckett and Soyinka is based on the premise that Beckett wrote before Soyinka and this therefore, creates the problem of determining the degree of the latter's artistic originality.

If Soyinka truly "aped" Western models, to what extent can one therefore, establish that he was influenced by any of them in the delineation of African customs, belief systems and worldviews? To what extent was he influenced by Western writers to project the absurdity of the human condition on the African continent? Is the question about human desolation and the quest for a veritable spiritual essence exclusively a European experience? It is only in an attempt to answer these questions that one comes to an understanding that writers of different continents, epochs and religions are confronted with similar situations of desolation and project similar spiritual visions which they demonstrate in literature. A close reading of Beckett's *Waiting for Godot* and Soyinka's *The Swamp Dwellers* from the perspective of myth critics like Jung, Frye and Kluckhohn shows a striking similarity in the playwrights' delineation of the human condition of desolate reality and the quest for salvation, yet remarkable contrasts in cultural and spiritual concepts and worldviews. With specific reference to religious opposition, Godwin Sogolo notes that:

> Anthropological speculations on the nature of African religious beliefs give the impression that religions in these cultures were of a peculiar sort, that is, that they were distinct in character from religions elsewhere in the world. (52)

This is quite evident in the oppositional cultural elements of which religion is an embodiment in Wole Soyinka's *The Swamp Dwellers* and Samuel Beckett's *Waiting for Godot*.

The issue that possibly motivates the link of Soyinka with Beckett is perhaps both playwrights' projection, in their different settings, of the casual link between human suffering and the possibilities of divine salvation which in the twentieth century was an issue of crucial importance. Both playwrights point to the fact that the excruciating human condition is a universal reality and that once created by his God no matter what form He takes, man is rendered desolate, abandoned to the fate of pain, hopelessness and languor. Commenting, for example, on the historical setting of *Waiting for Godot*, Declan Kiberd evokes the excruciating conditions of humanity represented by the tramps who,

> are presented as characters without much history, who are driven to locate themselves in the world with reference to geography. But the world in which they live has no overall structure, it is a dreadful place in which every moment is like the next.... Lacking an assured past, the tramps can have no clear sense of their own future.... They are waiting without hope for a deliverance from a being in whom they do not really believe (538-9).

Such a condition as described by Kiberd above expresses humanity's expedient need for salvation and this certainly is the dominant concern in Beckett's *Waiting for Godot* and *Endgame* and in Soyinka's *The Swamp Dwellers* and *The Road*. Soyinka on his part succeeds through the incorporation of the African idiom, myth and ritual from which perspective he explores the absurdity of the human condition against the background of African belief systems, while Beckett employs the modernist avant-garde theatrical techniques and Christian concepts to project the absurdity of human existence. In his most obscure plays Soyinka delineates life in complex textural frames, with equivalent complicated themes but in his simple works he is plain and lucid, in the manner of Beckett in *Waiting for Godot* which paradoxically have profound prophetic visions. The substance of *The Swamp Dwellers* can be evaluated within these realms. Because the play is almost devoid of an abstruse texture, un-native to Soyinka's art, its bare surface realism suggests almost nothing to a connoisseur with a voracious appetite for surface complexity. Apart from its apparent themes of the decay of a rural society the play above all reflects man's ultimate search for a veritable source of salvation for man. Since human life presents constant problems and contradictions, symbolised for example, by the setting of *The Swamp Dwellers,* the playwright finds the individual and the society in continual need of salvation for itself. This can be achieved either by mass act or through the dedication of earthly messiahs like Demoke in *A Dance of the Forests,* Eman in *The Strong Breed,* and Igwezu in *The Swamp Dwellers.*

Although there are perceptible differences in terms of regions, cultures and techniques between *Waiting for Godot* and *The Swamp Dwellers,* Beckett and Soyinka re-enact the situation of human predicament with artistic similitude. The similarity in terms of setting, characterisation, and themes among all others are quite evident in the two plays. The arid setting of Waiting for Godot which as Harold Hobson observes in the opening paragraph of his review "has nothing at all to seduce the senses" because its "drab bare scene is dominated by a withered a tree" (93). This is evocative of the rotting swamps and the dry North in *The Swamp Dwellers,* all of which are symbolic representations of the inexplicable and hazardous universe in which man finds himself. Beckett's indiscernible Godot represents Christian themes as James Acheson admits in his book, *Samuel Beckett's Artistic Theory and Practice,* while Soyinka's unappeasable Serpent is the spiritual essence in the swamps, an aspect of animism in African traditional religion. Beckett's desolate tramps Vladimir and Estragon who depend entirely on the arrival of Godot for salvation without whom they contemplate suicide echo in Soyinka's disillusioned Igwezu whose efforts to appease the Serpent to procure a happier life rather frustrates him.

The wealthy Pozzo parallels the capitalist Awuchike who takes advantage of man's wretchedness to exploit others. The uncompromising Lucky who is Pozzo's slave and the despised Beggar from the North are Sisyphean archetypes who readily submit themselves to their fates and who are determined to survive against all odds.

The central issue in both plays is on the question of salvation as stated above. Soyinka raises the problem as to whether or not the swamp dwellers should continue to depend on the Serpent for salvation in spite of the interminable calamities that confront them. *The Swamp Dwellers* projects this theme at a more individual level. It treats the story of a youth whose dependence on supernal assistance comes to no avail. His naivety, even leads him into terrible casualties which prompt him to question in the face of adversity, the authenticity of the god he worships. A closer appreciation of the play suggests the pertinence of the following question:

Should man continue to grope through an absurd existence with blind hope for divine salvation or should he seek other ways of saving himself ? This appears to be the playwright's obsession in the play. The protagonist of the play, Igwezu, an ideal son of the Swamps who is loyal to tradition, has performed all the necessary rites required by the deity to ensure a good harvest and a happy life with his wife. The impotence of this god gradually creeps into his awareness from several inexplicable mishaps that confront him, both in the city and the Swamps. In his short stay in the city to try his hands at making money, his twin brother, Awuchike, seduces his wife, contrary to the spiritual values of the Swamp. Much frustrating, he fails in his commercial enterprise. His misery is recalled later on his return to the Swamps when he tells the Kadiye: "I'm afraid I have had my turn already. I lost everything, my savings, even my standing as a man. I went into debt" (35). Igwezu's tragedy is more severe when he returns to the Swamps with the hope of recovering from his despair by harvesting his crops: "I came back with hope, with consolation in my heart. I came back with the assurance of one who has lived his land and tilled it faithfully (32). He discovers with utter disappointment and disbelief that the floods had ruined his farm and "the beans and the corn had made an everlasting pottage with the mud." Makuri's consolatory plea: "It is the will of the god," is least appealing to a man against whom fortune has turned her back. His reliance on the omnipotence of the Serpent begins to abate on being puzzled why he should be so righteous yet so forsaken. His contempt is explicit when he requires the Priest of the Serpent - the Kadiye, to give meaning to what seems "dark and sour." He achieves this through a series of clarification questions:

Igwezu: Did I not offer my goats to the Priest?
...And made it clear - that the offering was from me? That I demanded the protection of the heavens on me and my house, on my father and on my mother, on my wife, land and chattels?
Kadiye: All prayers were repeated.
Igwezu: And ever since I began to till the soil did I not give his due? Did I not bring the first lentils to the shrine, and pour the first oil upon the altar?
Kadiye: Regularly.
Igwezu: And when the Kadiye blessed my marriage and tied the heaven-made knot, did he not promise long life, did he not promise happiness?....
Kadiye: [Does not reply this time]. (Soyinka 38)

Igwezu's fate is the quintessence of man's misery in a world which offers no hopes of divine protection or signs of a promised land. His experience shows that dependence on divine assistance leads to more terrible adversity in life. On the other hand, Awuchike is the ungodly rewarded. Although he is physically absent in the play we gather from other characters that he denounces his parents, tradition and the Swamps with all its spiritual ramifications, commits a taboo and immerses himself in the rough city ways in which he thrives as a wealthy timber merchant. One gets obsessed at this point, why Igwezu should be forsaken and Awuchike rewarded.

We find this pattern of nihilism or the degenerating spiritual consciousness in Beckett's *Waiting for Godot* which as James Acheson suggests, "raises the question whether the modern man should or should not believe in divine salvation," although Acheson goes further to conclude that "Godot's non-arrival, strongly hints that he should not"(5). For Acheson, *Waiting for Godot* is an invective against Christian hope since the modern man, like Didi and Gogo wait endlessly for Godot who does not come. Although the tramps, Estragon and Vladimir, do not make any such effort as Igwezu does, they are victims of a scathing existence which they are unable to understand.

The characters in both plays, therefore, live a tragic and meaningless existence in which human experience is futile. In line with Declan Kiberd, Beryl Fletcher and John Fletcher maintain that the world of *Waiting for Godot* is "a world without divinity but a kind of malignant fate, a world in which man waits, hopes for something to give meaning to his life" (36). This is true of Vladimir and Estragon and Lucky and Pozzo, to a commendable extent. Estragon and Vladimir are trapped in the complications of life, a situation that is hopelessly unfathomable. They are unable to understand the *raison d'etre* for their existence. Existence seems to be something imposed on them by some unknown force and there is absolutely no meaning to it. Their very source of hope Godot is indefinable and unpredictable imposing on them the grim reality of desolation, what Estragon describes in the play as "dreadful privation" (11).

Lucky's fate is even more pathetic than any other in *Waiting for Godot*. The luggage he carries symbolises the burdens of the world carried by humanity. The rope tied to his neck and which Pozzo pulls at will is also symbolic of humanity's inability to extricate itself from the burdens of existence. Seen from Eugene Ngezem's viewpoint the burdens portray him as a victim of "arbitrary authority" which Pozzo incarnates (115). Pozzo as well, although seems comfortable at first, discovers himself blind one day. From the inevitable adversity that confronts him, he gradually comes to an understanding of the gruesome realities of existence in his remarks: "They gave birth astride a grave, the light gleams an instant, then it's night once more." (Beckett 89). The "grave" and "light" symbols represent death and life respectively. But the briefness in human life expressed in the symbolism reflects utter futility in human existence. Pozzo himself is symbolic of humanity that thinks itself free from the hazards of life but who sooner or later becomes a victim of fatal existence he cannot explain.

The characters in *The Swamp Dwellers* are confronted with similar ordeals as those in *Waiting for Godot*. The prime victim is Igwezu, an ideal son of the Swamps whose dependence on supernal assistance for a meaningful existence leads him to frustration. The impotence of his god gradually creeps into his awareness from several inexplicable mishaps that confront him both in the city and in the village of the Swamp. His venture in the city fails while his brother, Awuchike, who has severed all ties of family, religion and tradition, seduces his wife. His misery is recalled later on his return to the Swamps where he hopes to recover from his despair by harvesting his crops, but discovers with disappointment and anguish that the floods have ruined his farm. The idea of "loss" reflects Igwezu's inability to comprehend the complications of his existence, and therefore, questions and condemns the potency of the Serpent of the Swamps to whom he has offered enormous sacrifices:

> I know that the floods can come again. That the Swamps will continue to laugh at our endeavours. I know that we can feed the Serpent of the Swamps and kiss the Kadiye's feet but the vapours will still rise and corrupt the tassels of the corn. (Soyinka 39)

Doubts of divine competence to save humanity from the vagaries of life are revoked in his question:

> "If I slew the fatted calf, Kadiye, do you think the land may breathe again? If I slew all the cattle in the land and sacrificed every measure of goodness, would it make any difference to our lives, Kadiye? Would it make any difference to our fates?" (39).

The Kadiye, thus trapped and humiliated, leaves the scene threatening blood. But Igwezu's mind is now open. He has emancipated himself from the manacles of deceit, realising in a consolatory stand. "I know that we can appease the Serpent of the Swamps and kiss the Kadiye's feet, but the vapours will still rise and corrupt the tassels of the corn" (39). Igwezu's return to the city is manifest of the decision he has taken. The city symbolizes a place where a man who is aware that he is his own saviour struggles and succeeds as Awuchike does. Igwezu rejects the Swamps and all its spiritual values with the contention that, only the children and the old stay back in the village, in other words, only those who are ignorant or have not yet experienced the paradox of existence do not venture into the unknown.

His departure from the Swamps reflects that of his bondsman, the blind beggar who faces similar gruesome adversities: "I headed away from my home and set my face towards the river." The dry North from where he comes has undergone lengthy periods of draught, and later, a devastation of a crop-flourish by locusts, seems to show Soyinka's characteristic manner of presenting the poignant edges of life on which man is staked.

The plight of the blind Beggar from the North is even more severe than that of Igwezu, even though the latter is the protagonist of the play. Like Lucky, the blind Beggar undergoes all sorts of excruciating humiliation from people who show no sympathy for the afflicted, from natural hazards in the desert North including the "fly sickness" which eventually renders him blind, the severe droughts and the destruction of a rare flourishing of crops by locusts. As the Beggar narrates his ordeal to Makuri and his wife, Alu, at the initial stage of his blindness he believes that he can be rescued by his faith in Muhammad: "My faith promises paradise in the company of Muhammad and all the Prophets.... and then slowly the truth came to me, and I knew that I was living but blind" (15). The reality then is of the harrowing existence. Existence seems then to be imposed on the Beggar by a mysterious force which the Beggar identifies as Mohammad. The Beggar suffers for it because the paradise which Mohammad is supposed to procure for all believers is not attainable. The Beggar's southward journey is therefore, a rejection of his faith and a determination to till the soil wherever he finds fertile grounds. Makuri and Alu, in whose hut the action of *The Swamp Dwellers* takes place, are also victims of circumstances beyond their control. They understand that the destruction of the crops by floods and the disappearance of their sons, Igwezu and Awuchike, are the will of the Serpent who must not be questioned.

The understanding that things happen in both plays by chance and not by divine will as many other characters observe, is another source of grief for the characters. The issue of arbitrariness is explicit in *The Swamp Dwellers* where Igwezu and the Beggar, although righteous in conduct, are forsaken while Awuchike, Igwezu's twin brother who is full of impious actions, is rewarded. The situation of the two brothers Igwezu and Awuchike, as stated above is reminiscent of the fate of the thieves in the Bible whom Vladimir alludes to. Just as Igwezu questions the criterion for which divine competence punishes the righteous, and rewards the impious ones like Awuchike, the tramps impugn the basis for one of the thieves being saved and the other condemned:

Vladimir: Ah yes, the two thieves. Do you remember the story?
Estragon: No.
Vladimir: Shall I tell you? Estragon: No.

142

Vladimir: It'll pass time. (Pause.) Two thieves, crucified at the same time as our Saviour. One...
Estragon: Our what?
Vladimir: Our Saviour. Two thieves. One is supposed to have been saved and the other... (he searches for the contrary of saved)...damned. (12).

The inability to understand divine manifestation is the main source of despair in Beckett's *Godot*. Commenting on *Waiting for Godot* Eugene Webb states that,

The fate of the thieves, one of whom was saved and the other damned according to one of the four accounts that everybody believes, becomes as the play progresses a symbol of a condition of man in an unpredictable and arbitrary universe" (32).

The situation of arbitrariness or chance presupposes the silence or the absence of God, which provides more grounds for human misery.

The characters in both plays find themselves in the face of misery, an uncompromising situation without any defined pattern, highlighting chaos as the dominating force in the world with no question to be asked and no where to go. From an understanding of the gruesome realities of human existence, Samuel Beckett and Wole Soyinka see humanity in continual need for salvation. There are therefore, suggestions in Beckett's *Waiting for Godot* and Soyinka's *The Swamp Dwellers* that while in existence which origin is obscure, essence can be determined by individual choice and freewill, hence individual salvation. Salvation can also be attained through the benevolence of other persons; that is interpersonal or collective salvation. Furthermore, both playwrights do not completely ignore the presence of some spiritual essence in determining the fate of humanity.

The fact that human action, thought and vision in both plays are directed towards some ultimate reality is indicative of the possibility that divine salvation has a place in their being. Even if God's existence is doubtful as existentialists like Nietzsche and Jean-Paul Sartre show, man has indubitably created Him to give meaning to his own existence. This is reflected in man's eternal quest for some supernal being whom he thinks must be responsible for the existence of the marvels of the universe. Consequently, Beckett's Godot must be such a God created by Vladimir and Estragon, while the Serpent of the Swamps and Mohammad of the Muslim North must be patterns of beliefs created by people. The three religions may differ in concept and stature but they represent universal concerns and the verdict that all beliefs in the world culminate in a single search for the unknown. Through that quest, human life is patterned in more meaningful panoply of realities. At the level of individual salvation, some of the characters in the plays come to an understanding of their fates and in spite of the humiliation, to which they are subjected, make commendable efforts to survive in the face of adversity. Lucky in *Waiting for Godot* and the blind Beggar in *The Swamp Dwellers* stand out distinctly as representations of individual salvation.

Lucky, Pozzo's slave, unconditionally submits himself to the burdens of existence. He is certain however, that the residuals from his master's healthy existence are his. Pozzo tells Estragon who, like his friend Vladimir, is unable to do anything to save himself and who shows uncontrollable greed for the chicken bones thrown on the ground by Pozzo that, "in theory the bones go to the carrier" and the carrier of course is Lucky (Beckett 27). When asked why Lucky does not put down his luggage, Pozzo replies that "he wants to impress me so that I can keep him" (31). Similarly, Igwezu's bondsman, the Beggar from the dry North whose plight is even more severe because of his blindness is more conscious of the need to save himself rather than rely on external forces for salvation. His journey from the dry North to the swampy south is in search of a means of surviving. As a guest in Makuri's hut he indicates, against all entreaties by his host to beg like the others, his intention to till the soil where the earth is moist: "I wish to work on the soil. I wish to knead it between my fingers" (13).

This therefore, means that in the absence of a divine force that should take care of a desperate humanity, life is in the individual's own hands and he or she is responsible for it by the pattern of choices he or she makes. He is thrown to the dictates of chance but he must first show proof that he is directly responsible for his own life in an existence whose origin can hardly be satisfactorily explained. This is reflected in the Beggar's determination to till the soil though blind. All he needs is a patch of fertile ground by which means he can save himself. A noticeable link between the downtrodden Lucky and the Beggar is the element of revolt that does not necessarily tie them to their bondage, the kind of stubbornness which G.W.F. Hegel suggests "is that freedom which makes itself secure in a solid singleness, and keeps *within* the sphere of bondage" (244). Lucky does not execute every command given by his master, Pozzo and even Pozzo understands that Lucky has his own temperaments which must not be undermined. In the same light, the Beggar, in spite of the hospitality accorded him by Makuri and Alu, does not totally subject himself to their whims and caprices. He has his convictions and must pursue them to the end without giving the impression that he is completely helpless and cannot express his feelings freely. This way the two characters assert

145

their freedom to act as a means of saving their own lives not necessarily as acts of subjugation to bondage.

Soyinka's philosophy toes the line of Beckett's. The main difference, putting aside other factors, is in the psychological presentation of characters. Soyinka's hero makes considerable personal efforts to survive and all he seeks is the protection of the heavens over his achievements. On the contrary, Becketts's tramps are unable to do anything for themselves but wait for an illusory Godot to deliver salvation to them. In the end Godot does not come and tramps remain where they started, contemplating suicide as an alternative solution to their misery:

> Vladimir: We'll hang ourselves tomorrow (pause).
> Unless Godot comes.
> Estragon: And if he comes?
> Vladimir: We'll be saved. (Beckett 94)

Both works further demonstrate the fact that in addition to attempts by the individual to save himself, people can rely on the resources of each other for a more meaningful existence. The problem of Estragon's hunger is temporarily solved when Vladimir offers him a carrot. At the instant, Estragon realises that their salvation does not necessarily depend on Godot:

> Estragon: (his mouth full, vacuously) We're not
> Tied!....
> Vladimir: How do you mean tied? Estragon: Down.
> Vladimir: But to whom, by whom? Estragon: To your man.
> Vladimir: To Godot? Tied to Godot? What idea! No question of it. (
> Pause) For the moment (Beckett 20-21).

Estragon's and Vladimir's worldview here illustrates that God represented by Godot in this sense is important only when humanity is in trouble. Estragon realises at this point the importance of another fellow human in solving problems. Godot instantly becomes insignificant to Estragon when his mouth is full with carrots, when he is sure of his survival even if it were temporarily so. Estragon in particular is an archetype of the hypocritical Christian who looks for God only to solve his immediate personal problems and once that problem is solved the notion of God is obliterated. He represents the Western man who Nietzsche lambastes in the parable of the mad man who declared the death of God. Nietzsche's startling statement that God was dead meant that humankind no longer believed in God. Humankind had destroyed his faith in God, in other words, they killed God (Nietzsche 95-96). In the same way, Estragon's faith in Godot abates as soon as he achieves his basic needs. Vladimir however realises that their extrication from Godot is just a temporary matter. In the same way, Lucky essentially depends on Pozzo for survival. Put in another way, there exists a mutual dependence between Pozzo and Lucky that is advantageous to the developing consciousness of Lucky. The antithetical natures of Pozzo and Lucky manifestly become a synthesis of master and slave. He carries his burden uncomplaining in order to benefit from the chicken bones thrown on the ground by Pozzo. Lucky is aware of Pozzo's dependency on a slave and this illustrates why he does not execute all instructions. His salvation is dependent on Pozzo but also on his self-consciousness and although Pozzo subjects him to the most excruciating humiliation, Lucky's helplessness is not as manifest as that of the idle Vladimir and Estragon. Alexandre Kojeve puts us in the existential mind of Lucky to demonstrate that the contradictions within him are phenomenal, for as he writes, "in *this* world everything is slavery, and the master is as much a slave here as he is" (55).

In *The Swamp Dwellers*, the Beggar's Christlike presence stands as symbol of expiation and enlightenment. His brilliant suggestions about land reclamation are intended to guide the indigenes on how to solve the problem of flood without relying on external forces. As Igwezu's mentor, he prompts him to discover the venality of the Kadiye and also his own naivety. The Beggar's ideas in the play represent Soyinka's ideals of individual lone-act-of-courage in the effort of saving humanity whenever such an individual possesses the will and the resources. Eldred Jones writes that:

> this act of salvation is not a mass act; it comes about through the vision and the dedication of individuals who doggedly pursue their vision in spite of the opposition of the very society they seek to save (12).

This is the essential role of the Beggar in the play. Although Makuri considers his insistent propositions of land reclamation as "profanities," the Beggar goes on to enforce the idea and as Igwezu's mentor prompts him to denounce the spirituality of the Swamps and come to self-awareness of survival by individual effort. The Beggar's intervention rescues Igwezu and the rest of the dwellers from hopeless dependence on the Serpent, although not without meeting with resistance from Igwezu's parents, Makuri and his wife Alu, who have committed themselves to an unflinching reverence of the Serpent.

The hospitality shown towards the Beggar by Makuri and his wife, when he arrives in their hut in the Swamps reflects another dimension of interpersonal salvation which is often rooted in what is commonly referred to as "African hospitality," whereby the sorrows and joys of an individual are shared by other members of the community. Makuri's sympathy towards the stranger is quite explicit. He calls him the "afflicted of the gods" and his wife washes the mud on the Beggar's feet, dries them then rubs with ointment, an action borrowed from the anointing of the feet of Jesus by the Magdalene.

The examples above, of interpersonal salvation illustrate the existentialist idea that man is the future of man in the sense that man's problems in an ailing universe can partly be solved through the initiative and the benevolence of his fellow man. But once humanity is conscious of its commitment to individual, interpersonal or collective efforts to make existence tolerable, there is also a need to impose a spiritual pattern on its existence, whether it is traditional African, Christian or Islamic. To a critic like John Leeland Kundert-Gibbs, "hope or expectation springs from a sense of lack, emptiness or insecurity" (58). He consequently identifies Godot with the void at the centre of being in his Zen Buddhism and Chaos theory. Following his theory therefore, it is neither the Zen Buddhism, nor Godot, nor the Serpent of the Swamps, nor Muhammad that imposes its essence on humanity but humanity's yearning to fill a void by imposing a spiritual pattern on itself. By imposing a divine pattern on themselves, Vladimir and Estragon achieve some degree of meaning, what Eugene Webb describes as "an illusory, but desperately defended pattern" (26). In *The Swamp Dwellers,* Makuri and Alu also impose a spiritual prototype on themselves. They are die-hard worshippers of the Serpent and the Beggar's brilliant idea on land reclamation would hardly shaken their faith in the Serpent because their dependence on the Serpent, even with the accompanying casualties, is what still gives meaning to their lives. They confirm John Mbiti's claim that

in their traditional life African peoples are deeply religious. It is religion, more than anything else, which colours their understanding of the universe and their empirical participation in that universe, making life a profoundly religious phenomenon (262).

If Beckett disavows God in conformity with the philosophical theorising of Friedrich Nietzsche, Jean-Paul Sartre and even James Acheson, there is evidence that there is a possibility of the existence of divine essence whose nature is unpredictable and whose ways are inexplicit. This God either exists and does not care or is the invention of man to give pattern and meaning to his life. Beckett and Soyinka therefore, share in thinking with Martin Heiddeger, Nietzsche and Jean-Paul Sartre that without depending on external sources man's life should be determined by the pattern of choices he makes; with Husserl and Søren Kierkegaard that man cannot completely dismiss the possibility of supernal assistance in the determination of human fate. Religion, in all regions and in all epochs, tends to have an organic life of its own which recognises the existence of divine activity and man's response to it no matter what form it takes (Idowu 203). However, such existence placed entirely on divine benevolence renders it more excruciating, like in the case of Vladimir and Estragon because Godot does not come in the end and they are unable to do anything to help themselves. Although Gunter Andres argues that the waiting in the case of Vladimir and Estragon, is just an incessant attempt to make time pass which is so characteristic, and which reflects the specific misery and absurdity of their life" the fact that Beckett pits them against

Lucky who finds meaning in his life by subjecting himself to Pozzo is self explicit (147-148).

Critics like Gerald Moore and Ulli Beier who see African theatre only in terms of texture and its peculiarity to the African continent miss the point. The straightforward nature of *The Swamp Dwellers* is more complex than one would expect. The play is more substantial in terms of the overall philosophical vision than some of the abstruse volumes which have conferred upon its author all his excellence. Attempts should be made to link patterns and situations with universal human experience as this study of Beckett and Soyinka demonstrates. As Simon Gikandi argues, African writers do not have social functions or responsibilities which are different from their counterparts elsewhere in the world. Gerald Moore's assessment of *The Swamp Dwellers* as "least substantial" (16) is, therefore, inadequate. David Cook's opinion is that the ideas in the play are "dramatically projected with great simplicity but with great force" (118). Joel Adedeji states that "Soyinka uses the theatre to make statements of human needs and values" such as *The Swamp Dwellers* illustrates (127). These needs and values are not limited to the Nigerian or African experience but to the universal human experience. Soyinka achieves this in some of his very revealing plays like *The Road, Madmen and Specialists,* and *The Swamp Dwellers* which, in the opinion of. Acholonu, "often call to mind the language, style and themes of the plays of Albert Camus, Jean-Paul Sartre and above all those of Samuel Beckett" (14).

It is however evident from this analysis that while Beckett in his own region and era saw the human condition from a purely Western perspective and belief pattern, Soyinka projects same from an African domain. Both playwrights converge at a point where, as Clyde Kluckhohn thinks, the "same general order" is reached.

Chapter Eight

The Existential Maturation

E.Grayson

ALTHOUGH J.M. Coetzee's *Disgrace* has garnered a great deal of critical attention in the six years since its publication, most critical literature written about Coetzee's novel attempts to identify and delineate a process by which the protagonist David Lurie lifts himself out of a state of disgrace, often claiming that a condition of grace is the former professor's ultimate destination. Yet, as Ron Charles observes, the moment one begins to consider the nature of Lurie's (dis)grace, "the novel's title begins to refract meaning in a dozen directions" (20). Furthermore, commentators continue to struggle with what Gareth Cornwell calls "the fertile indirections of its narrative style" ("Disgraceland" 43.) Indeed, combined with Coetzee's deceptively simple prose, *Disgrace* has encouraged a range of equally convincing, yet widely divergent, interpretations. In their discussions of (dis)grace, critics have viewed Lurie as a burgeoning Stoic, a man threatened by emasculation, and an individual suffering from a lack or intimacy while positing that the novel depicts the attainment of grace through "secular humility" (Kissack and Titlestad 135) and the struggle to remain human in an inhumane world. However, despite the novel's concern with states of (dis)grace, the trajectory David Lurie's life takes during the course of the novel might be better understood as a process of existential maturation. Rather than chart the fall and subsequent redemption of a "mighty" academic, as Melanie Isaacs's father sardonically remarks, *Disgrace* documents the end of David Lurie's reluctant acceptance of aging and mortality (Coetzee 167). In fact, Lurie's strikingly powerful fixation on mortality not only girds the aforementioned readings, but may also explain the "odd kink in [the novel's] narrative structure," namely what "the first quarter of the story [has] to do with what follows" (Hynes 1). It is only after David Lurie acknowledges and internalises his own eventual mortality that he discovers anything akin to grace. Indeed, Lurie's period of existential maturation, his gradual acceptance of life's eventualities, also marks a period of creative self- discovery during which Lurie finds his voice as he composes a comic opera "that will never be performed" (215). *Disgrace*, then, may be read as David Lurie's journey from estrangement to sexual, creative and existential self-actualization.

The first quarter of the novel, rather than depict Lurie's tumble into disgrace as many commentators have suggested, presents us with a man who has been isolated from, and disengaged with, the world for some time already. Tellingly, *Disgrace* opens with Lurie thinking that "[f]or a man of his age, fifty-two, divorced, he has, to his mind, solved the problem of sex rather well" (1). Since Lurie regards physical intimacy as a problem which must be solved as one would fill in a crossword puzzle or balance a budget, we may infer that, for him, sex is little more than a chore he must perform periodically. In other words, Lurie's sex life lacks the sort of emotional intimacy one would assume he enjoyed as a married man. Furthermore, the line reveals Lurie's acute awareness that ageing will only make solving the problem increasingly difficult. Thus, as Michael Gorra observes, Coetzee's opening line only "tells us that David Lurie hasn't solved the problem at all" (7). Thus, Lurie's relationship with a prostitute named Soraya only reveals the inadequacy of physical intimacy to satiate his hunger for emotional intimacy.

Although Lurie claims "that ninety minutes a week of a woman's company are enough to make him happy, who used to think he needed a wife, a home, a marriage" and that "[h]is needs turn out to be quite light after all, light and fleeting," he nevertheless longs for a different arrangement with Soraya (5). Indeed, Lurie admits to having developed "an affection" for Soraya that "[t]o some degree, he believes…is reciprocated" (2). Yet, despite his apparent rejection of emotional attachment, Lurie indulges his need to share his life with Soraya:

> During their sessions he speaks to her with a certain freedom, even on occasion unburdens himself. She knows the facts of his life. She has heard the stories of his two marriages, knows about his daughter and his daughter's ups and downs. She knows many of his opinions. (3)

Despite his emotional investment in the relationship, however, Soraya "reveals nothing" about her life or her true identity outside of the escort service employing her (3). Still, Lurie "has toyed with the idea of asking her to see him in her own time," indicating that he harbours a desire to establish a relationship with the prostitute that does not rely on his pecuniary support to subsist, one founded upon the mutual affection he senses in their interactions. Yet, Lurie develops "a shrewd idea of how prostitutes speak among themselves about the men who frequent them, the older men in particular" and fears that Soraya secretly finds him repugnant

(8). Clearly, Lurie is acutely aware of his age-reduced sexual vitality, a fact that depresses him tremendously. Whereas "his height, his good bones, his olive skin, his flowing hair" had resulted in an attractive appearance that had long been "the backbone of his life," Lurie despairs because "[w]ithout warning his powers fled" along with his youth (7). Dreading the day when "he will be shuddered over" by women like Soraya, Lurie hopes he can establish a relationship with the prostitute in order to stave off the inevitable period when one must "turn one's mind to the proper business of the old: preparing to die" (8-9). In other words, Lurie does not merely wish to solve "the problem of sex" with the prostitute, he also seeks "[s]omeone to count on when the worst arrives: the fall in the bathroom, the blood in the stool" (60). The perseverance of thoughts pertaining to the process of aging also contributes to Lurie's feelings of disconnectedness in his vocational life. Professionally, Lurie had been a professor of modern languages until the Cape Town University College became Cape Technical University under the sweeping reforms of "the great rationalization" which cut the Departments of Classics and Modern Languages (3). Thus, when we first encounter Lurie, he is not the "mighty" professor Mr. Isaacs suggests he may once have been, but rather a disgruntled adjunct professor of communications, thoroughly disinterested in the generic "Communication Skills" courses he teaches (3). Yet, despite having "no respect for the material he teaches," Lurie finds that his students' "indifference galls him more than he will admit," a sentiment that suggests the professor longs to establish an intellectual connection with his students (4). In other words, the fact that Lurie's students "look right through him when he speaks" and "forget his name" further isolates the professor from the world he inhabits.

As his sense of estrangement intensifies, Lurie continues blaming the aging process for his discomfort, notably in his futile effort to share his admiration of William Wordsworth with the students taking his Romantic Poetry course. Facing the "[b]lank incomprehension" of the students sitting before him, Lurie despairs at his inability to "bring them to him" (22). Hoping to spark interest in his lecture, Lurie inserts a discussion of romantic love into his talk despite having wondered if "the young still fall in love" or if "that mechanism [is] obsolete by now, unnecessary, quaint" (13). Sensing that "[h]e is out of touch" with the younger generation to whom he lectures, Lurie imagines that the students wonder "[w]hat does this *old* man know about love?" (13, 22; italics Coetzee's). Thus, aging has become something of a scapegoat for David Lurie. Although he openly declares himself "no great shakes as a teacher," Lurie seems eager to blame his age for his inability to reach young students (63). In other words, the first quarter of the novel informs us that David Lurie attributes his social and professional isolation to external, temporal factors. The remaining three-quarters of the novel, then, follow Lurie through a series of traumatic events which force him to accept his fate and, in turn, enable Lurie to find a voice with which to express his innermost concerns.

Critics such as Derek Attridge may claim that David is "[f]orced to resign from the university" in a state of disgrace, however, the novel suggests that by the time Cape Technical University dismisses Lurie for having initiated an affair with Melanie Isaacs, he no longer wishes to teach at the university anyway (102). One is apt to suggest that Lurie leaves Cape Town less in a state of disgrace than in a state of mingled despair and disgust. Disgusted by the "emasculated" state of academia and "tired of criticism, tired of prose measured by the yard," Lurie feels "more out of place than ever" as an academic (4). Coupled with his aforementioned dejection at the ever-hastening approach of his old age, the university's discharge of David Lurie seems more a desired respite than a punitive measure.If anything, Lurie's pursuit of and subsequent affair with Melanie Isaacs seems more a catalyst for the inevitable "clearing of the decks" Lurie must undertake in order to adjust to old age than simply the rash indiscretion most commentators believe it to be (9). Even as he pursues Soraya, Lurie senses that "[h]e ought to give up, retire from the game" lest he join the ranks of lecherous "tramps and drifters...clinging to the last to their place at the sweet banquet of the senses" (9, 24). Yet, he abolishes any such scruple from his mind, electing to indulge in one "last leap of the flame of sense before it goes out," knowing full well that he risks sparking a scandal and ending his career (27). That Lurie believes his affair with Melanie to be the "last leap of the flame of sense" indicates that he believes his existence as the epicentre of "an anxious flurry of promiscuity" has run its course (7). Indeed, as the scandal breaks, Lurie has little difficulty acknowledging the veracity of Rosalind's assertion that "it is the right of the young to be protected from the sight of their elders in the throes of passion" (44). Lurie's decision to conduct an affair with Melanie, then, may be read as a deliberate capping-off of David's middle age, a transitional event which both exalts in and irrevocably closes a stage in the professor's life.

The novel's shift in locale from urban Cape Town to Lucy Lurie's rural smallholding outside Grahamstown in South Africa's Eastern Cape marks David's uncomfortable first steps into the unfamiliar territory of old age. However, while most critics locate the origins of Lurie's burgeoning humility in what Linda Seidel calls David's "symbolic impotence" during the gang rape episode, I would suggest that the scene is perhaps equally significant for marking "the first time he has a taste of what it will be like to be an old man, tired to the bone, without hopes, without desires, indifferent to the future" (107). Although Charles Savran argues that this moment marks Lurie's redemption, *Disgrace* seems to suggest that this point merely represents the nadir of David Lurie's journey towards self- understanding. In fact, Lurie feels "he has begun to float toward his end...it fills him with (the word will not go away) despair" (107-08). It is not until he returns to Cape Town that he finally makes peace with mortality and finds a sense of purpose in life, through music.

During his meeting with Melanie Isaacs's family in George, Lurie explains that the young woman "struck up a fire in me" but that "when I burn, I don't sing" (166, 171). Interestingly, Lurie's rather opaque explanation recalls his earlier opinion when expressing his dissatisfaction with the underlying assumptions of the Communications Department at Cape Technical University. In Lurie's "own opinion, which he does not air...the origins of speech lie in song and the origins of song in the need to fill out with sound the overlarge and rather empty human soul" (4). Thus, Lurie simultaneously acknowledges the emptiness of his affair with Melanie while hinting at the role music will play in his own self-discovery.

Throughout *Disgrace*, David Lurie exhibits what Jacqueline Rose calls "a state of mind characterized by...a failure to connect" with the world and a paralysing inability to articulate the despair he feels as an essentially friendless aging man (192). However, upon returning to Cape Town, Lurie resumes the chamber opera he had attempted to write about Lord Byron's life in Italy. Initially attracted to the libertine lifestyle Byron celebrated during his life, Lurie plans on basing his "chamber-play about love and death" on the rake's torrid love affair with the young Contessa Teesa Guiccioli (180). However, Lurie soon discovers that only "an older Teresa" will "engage his heart as his heart is now" (181). Thus, as Zoë Wicomb observes, an aging Teresa appeals to Lurie because "like Byron's abandoned mistress, he is concerned about ageing and sexuality" (217). As Lurie continues working on the chamber-play, "he begins to live his days more fully" (183). With exuberance hitherto foreign to Lurie, the former professor finds his growing affection for the "woman past her prime, without prospects" changes the entire scope of his project (182). Whereas Lurie had initially intended to rely upon the sombre timbre of a grand piano to give voice to the lovers, he soon discovers that an "odd little seven-string banjo" he had purchased for Lucy when she was a child actually expresses the Contessa's emotions perfectly (184). James Hynes claims that "Coetzee seems to lack...a profound sense of comedy" and cannot find "absurdity even in the direst situations." However it is precisely the comic aspect of Lurie's chamber-play that marks his turn towards an existential acceptance of mortality (1). Indeed, Lurie expresses pleasant surprise upon realizing that "[i]t is not the erotic that is calling to him, nor the elegiac, but the comic" (184). For Lurie, then, the "flat, tiny slap" of the "ludicrous instrument" enables him to laugh at a situation similar to his own (184-85). Significantly, as he draws the "plink-plonk-plunk" out of the banjo, he reflects "[s]o this is art...and this is how it does its work! How strange! How fascinating!" (185). By expressing his surprise, Lurie reveals that, despite having devoted "a career stretching back a quarter of a century" to the study of art, he has never truly understood the creative impulse (4). In other words, finding the comedy in the Contessa's otherwise tragic existence has freed his creative voice, a development which immediately results in a newfound appreciation for and participation in life.

Prior to David Lurie's discovery of comedy in the Contessa's story, the professor had been reluctant to interpret the circumstances of his own life in any but the harshest of terms. After laughter enters Lurie's life, however, he also experiences the contentment that he lacks throughout the majority of Disgrace. Whereas he clearly resents the winding down of his sex life earlier in the novel, Lurie's "heart floods with thankfulness" when he reflects on his amorous liaisons at the novel's close (192). Furthermore, Lurie begins expressing a more relaxed understanding of aging and mortality. Rather than regard old age as a grotesque struggle to live with bloody stool, "cracked false teeth and hairy ear holes," Lurie accepts ageing as a natural part of existence (24). When Rosalind harangues him for having thrown away his life, suggesting that Lurie may "end up as one of those sad old men who poke around in rubbish bins," he replies that he will simply "end up in a hole in the ground" like everyone else (189). Furthermore, in addition to enabling Lurie to accept death calmly as an inevitable part of life, the shift in Lurie's attitude towards mortality also allows him to find humour in his own condition. When a group of children from D Village happen to pass him as he sits among the dogs at the clinic, he revels in the comic story he imagines his behaviour will inspire: "What a tale to tell back home: a mad old man who sits among the dogs singing to himself !" (212).

As Lurie grows to accept his own aging and eventual death, he also begins to empathize with the animals he and Bev Shaw regularly put to sleep at the clinic. At the time Lurie begins working at the clinic, Bev Shaw claims to sense that he likes animals, an assertion to which Lurie sardonically replies "I eat them, so I suppose I must like them, some parts of them" (81).

By the novel's conclusion, however, Lurie is prepared to give the dogs "what he no longer has difficulty in calling by its proper name: love" (219). Having come to terms with the omnipresence and, in a sense, omnipotence of death through laughter, Lurie finally attains a variety of connectedness with the world by assisting Bev Shaw as she performs euthanasia. In a sense, Lurie's acceptance of his own proximity to death enables him to form the sort of emotional concern for the dogs that he could not achieve in his relationships with Soraya or Melanie. Whereas Soraya's secrecy and Melanie's youth, among other factors, prevent Lurie from establishing a connection with either woman, the dogs' imminent death presents a situation with which Lurie immediately identifies and, consequently, elicits genuine emotion. This love, while directed at the dogs, actually allows Lurie to recover the sense of connectedness he has lacked throughout Disgrace by enabling him to form a bond with Bev Shaw, the only person who can truly understand the gravity of their situation.

Coetzee concludes *Disgrace* with a rather ambiguous scene in which David Lurie chooses not to forestall Bev Shaw's killing of a crippled dog with which he has formed an attachment. Nevertheless, the novel's final scene does reaffirm Lurie's reengagement with society. The concluding episode, while bleak, presents David Lurie as a motivated and even compassionate part of a social unit. That Lurie's new vocation deals exclusively in canine and feline euthanasia only emphasizes the remarkable process of existential maturation he undergoes throughout Disgrace. David Lurie may not achieve the grace J.M. Coetzee's title seems to imply, but the professor does attain a state of being equally foreign to the protagonist at the novel's start, a sense of peace.

Chapter Nine

African Modernity

B.M'Baye

IN *The Black Atlantic* (1993), Paul Gilroy argues that, from the late eighteenth century to the present, the cultures of Blacks in the West have been hybrid and antithetical to "ethnic absolutism" (4-5). According to Gilroy, the modern history of the Black Atlantic is a discontinuous trajectory in which countries, borders, languages, and political ideologies are crossed in order to oppose "narrow nationalism" (12). Gilroy's term "Black Atlantic" describes the "rhizomorphic, fractal structure of the transcultural, international formation" of modern Black cultures that oppose the nationalist focus "common to English and African American versions of cultural studies" (4). Gilroy defines "modernity" as the period from the end of the eighteenth to the beginning of the nineteenth centuries when the ideas of "nationality, ethnicity, authenticity, and cultural integrity" that sustain contemporary cultural studies in the West were first developed (2). Gilroy writes:

> The conspicuous power of these modern subjectivities and the movements they articulated has been left behind. Their power has, if anything, grown, and their ubiquity as a means to make political sense of the world is currently paralleled by the languages of class and socialism by which they once appeared to have been surpassed.

My concern here is less with explaining their longevity and
enduring appeal than with exploring some of the special political
problems that arise from the fatal junction of the concept of
nationality with the concept of culture and the affinities and
affiliations which link the Blacks of the West to one of their
adoptive, parental cultures: the intellectual heritage of the West. (2)

There are problematic aspects of Gilroy's concept of
Black modernity. The first element is Gilroy's representation
of the essentialising or romanticising of Black culture as
being antithetical to modernity. The second is Gilroy's
definition of Black modernity as simply a Western
phenomenon, as if Africans and other Blacks from the non-
western hemisphere had not produced valuable cultures and
identity formations that fit popular notions of the modern. The
third aspect is Gilroy's exclusion of the role that African
intellectuals played in the international forms of nationalism
and resistance movements that Gilroy found to be central in
the history of the Black Atlantic and Black modernity.
Conceiving Black modernity and the Black Atlantic as
referring only to intellectual, cultural, historical, or
technological developments in the African American and the
Caribbean West is reductive and simplistic. The danger in
such a rationale is the failure to validate the intricate
relationships between Blacks of Africa in the West and those
who have been in the Diaspora since slavery times, and those
between tradition and modernity. In *The African Imagination:
Literature in Africa and the Black Diaspora* (2001), Abiola
Irele writes:

> African literature may be said to derive an immediate interest
> from the testimony it offers of the preoccupation of our
> writers with the conflicts and dilemmas involved in the
> tradition/modernity dialectic. This observation is based on the
> simple premise that, as with many other societies and cultures in the

so-called Third World, the impact of Western civilization on Africa has occasioned a discontinuity in forms of life throughout the continent. It points to the observation that the African experience of modernity associated with a Western paradigm is fraught with tensions at every level of the communal existence and individual apprehension. (ix)

Irele's statement suggests the big problem in how African culture and literature are often interpreted from Western notions of modernity that do not appreciate the African-centred idea of stable traditions. Alternatively, Abiola proposes a concept of modernity that acknowledges the continuous experimentation with new forms of expressions that negotiate in harmonious ways with old ones. Irele writes,

Significantly, the idea of tradition has featured prominently in the process, both as theme and as determining factor of the very form of our modern expression. Above all, the idea of tradition has served us essentially as a focus of consciousness and imagination and thus enabled us to formulate a vision of our place in the world. (67)

Two aspects of *Ambiguous Adventure* emerge by using similar conceptions of the relation between tradition and modernity in African literature. First is the book's representation of the experiences of the protagonist Samba Diallo in both Africa and France. The second is the book's depiction of Black cultural nationalism as a consistent element of African-centred notions of modernity and modernization. As Kane's novel shows, modern Blacks can embrace both their hybrid and authentic experiences and identities while demanding that (1) Europeans acknowledge the humanity of Black people and that (2) they repair the consequences of their colonization of African lands and people.

Africa in Gilroy's Concept of the Black Atlantic

Gilroy's concept of the Black Diaspora (or of the Black Atlantic) refers mainly to Black experiences in the United States, London, and to a degree in the Caribbean. The concept of "Diaspora," which is often used interchangeably with that of the Black Atlantic, comes from the Greek word *diaspeirein* (to spread about). It was traditionally applied to the dispersion of Jews outside Israel after the sixth century B.C. In the twentieth century, the term has been enlarged to include the dispersal of Africans in New World societies by historical forces such as slavery and imperialism (Bonnett and Watson 2). According to Gilroy, the "Black Atlantic" intellectual resistance began as a broad nationalist movement started by Blacks in England and America in the eighteenth and nineteenth centuries. Gilroy brilliantly explores the activism or writings of Black nationalists of the West such as the eighteenth century Black British Robert Weddeburn and William Davidson, whose radicalism and fight against racial oppression he validates and explores in depth. In 1778, Wedderburn, who was a freed mulatto and the child of a slave dealer named James Wedderburn, migrated to London at the age of seventeen (12). In London, Wedderburn published ultra-radical tracts in which he described the horror of slavery and the right of the Caribbean slave to slay his master. Wedderburn was tried for blasphemy when he promised to write home to Kingston and "tell them to murder their masters as soon as they please" (12). Wedderburn was later acquitted when he persuaded an English jury that his words were not sedition but a mere practice of the "true and infallible genius of prophetic skill" (12). Soon after his release, Wedderburn and his associate William Davidson became active participants in the

Marylbone Reading Society, an ultra-radical Black subculture group formed in 1819 after the Peterloo Massacre. Wedderburn and Davidson were Black British navy recruits to whom the experience of slavery provided a motive for developing an ideology of liberty and justice for Blacks of the Diaspora.

According to Gilroy, like Wedderburn and Davidson, the African American Martin Robinson Delany was a strong voice for Black liberty and justice. In the 1858, Delany was one of the officers of the National Board Commissioners, an organization that aimed at preparing the return of African Americans to Africa. Throughout the last half of the nineteenth century, Delany called for unity among Blacks of the world. In *The Condition* (1852), Delany pointed out that, in all ages, national groups such as the Hungarians, the Scotch, the Irish, the Welsh, the Jews, and the Russians have had the natural desire to maintain their national characteristics "in hopes of seeing the day when they may return to their former national position of self- government and independence let that be in whatever part of the habitable world it may be" (Gilroy 23).

While he recognises the importance of African-British and African American nationalists in the formation of Black modernist thought, Gilroy fails to represent the contributions of African intellectuals to this tradition. Apart from his very thin discussions of the *Négritude* movement, Gilroy practically leaves African intellectuals out of his focus. *Négritude* is a literary and political movement founded in 1932 in Paris by expatriate African intellectuals such as Léopold Sédar Senghor, Aimé Césaire, and Leon Gontran Dumas. The goal of Négritude was to assert the power and beauty of Black culture through art and literature, and to demand the political and cultural independence of Africans (Chowdhury 36).

Moreover, Gilroy mentions how the formation of the journal *Presence Africaine* in 1947, which was spearheaded by the Senegalese philosopher Alioune Diop, "was an important moment in the developing awareness of the African Diaspora as a transnational and intercultural multiplicity" (195). He also suggests how the second Congress of Negro Writers and Artists, held in Rome in 1959, was a determining moment when Richard Wright and the Negritude writers agreed, at least in the published proceedings, "that the unity of culture was not to be guaranteed by the enduring force of a common African heritage" (195). Gilroy credits the proceedings of the conference for defining "the colonial experience" as "an additional source of cultural synthesis and convergence"(195). Gilroy, however, deplores what he perceived as the actual sense of mystified unity and ragged anti- colonialism which emerged among the black scholars by the end of the conference₁. Gilroy then minimizes the cultural and political importance of the anti-colonialism put forth in the agenda of *Presence Africaine* and the Rome conference. By representing such movements as cultural and political essentialisms, Gilroy denies their relevance in modernity. Gilroy's failure to suggest the relevance of such movements in the struggles of modernity reflects the narrowness of his concept of "Black Diaspora."

Colonization and Modernity in *Ambiguous Adventure*

Ambiguous Adventure (1962) is a historical and autobiographical novel written by a Senegalese author who lived on different sides of the Atlantic Ocean and who examined the change and dilemma that the contact between France and Africa brought into the cultures of Africans at home and abroad. The book is an essential work of African history because, as Irele has pointed out, it takes us "back to the early years of French occupation in Sahelian West Africa to the period of transition between the dissolution of the precolonial Islamic states in the region and the full establishment of the French colonial administration as the point of departure of the narrative" (*African* 87). In the book, Kane captures the transformation, anxieties, and ambivalence that colonization created in the lives of modern Africans as the latter attempted to define their identities and understand the nature of their relationships to the West. Drawing from the social, political, and cultural contexts of his upbringing in northern Senegal and of his expatriate years in France, Kane fictionalized the consequences that geographic displacement and fragmentation of Black identity created in the lives of modern Africans. This disintegration of Black identity was not alien to Kane himself because, like his hero Samba, he came from the noble and predominantly Islamic people of northern Senegal known as the *Diallobé*. Like Samba, Kane was sent to French school when he was about 10 years old, studied philosophy at a university in Paris, and returned home with an acute sense of the disillusionment that colonization had created in the mind of the educated African whose culture and humanity westerners represented as inferior. When he was asked why he wrote *Ambiguous Adventure*, Kane replied:

> [I] was pushed by the desire to say that our societies had in themselves a profound reality. That any desire to assimilate them was an error since they have their own basic civilization. It was to justify colonization that the Europeans pretended that we were not human beings. On this basis also they contested the validity of our cultural values. But this attitude wasn't consistent with reality[2].

In his attempt to explain the history of European misperception and transformation of African cultures, Kane writes a novel in which Samba (which was the author's "house-name"), goes to France and finds that he cannot identify with western concepts of development and Africanity. Yet, in France, Samba also realizes that he cannot easily return to the stable African Islamic and cultural traditions that had produced him. Thierno, who used to be Samba's Coranic teacher in the Diallobé country, gets sick and dies in the absence of his former loyal student. Summoned by his father, Samba arrives to the country of the Diallobé late and, on account of being acculturated and lost in philosophical meditations, refuses to kneel and pray in front of his teacher's grave. It is at this unexpected moment that the character of Le Fou (the Madman), who had been Thierno's assistant during Samba's absence, stabs Samba to death. The exact cause of Samba's death is the most enduring philosophical question in African literature. Samba's death epitomizes the difficulty of knowing "how can the old values survive?" which Oscar Ronald Darthorne asks in his 1974 tribute to Kane.[3]

Yet Samba's death also symbolizes the hard task of knowing how to find a balance between African and Western values. As evident in W. E. B. Du Bois's concept of Double-Consciousness, the attempt to walk a fine line between African and Western cultures is a dilemma that African Americans and other Blacks of the Diaspora have experienced throughout history[4].

By 1890, Europeans had colonized most of Africa. The emancipation of African Americans in 1865 contrasted with the institution of a new form of slavery in Africa. From the 1880s to the 1960s, France, Britain, and Portugal took the land of Africans and forced the people to work for the prosperity of Europe[5]. The dispossessed Africans witnessed

170

the disintegration of their social lives as Europeans took their freedom and compelled them to work for the benefit of a foreign hegemonic power that had no other goal but to exploit African labour and raw materials. Like slavery, colonization was then a brutal phase in the history of Blacks, since it invokes the incalculable damage Europeans have inflicted on Africans.

In *Ambiguous Adventure*, Kane depicts the impact of colonization on Africans through the eyes of Samba Diallo, the major character who witnesses the social and economic collapse in his native Diallobé country on the first day when the French invaded it. The French colonization of the Diallobé began one morning in the 1880s when the Diallobé people woke up under the sound of canons announcing their forced subordination to the law and order of France. That morning, the Diallobé saw how their land was being robbed by the French with such a striking mix of unimaginable violence and terror. Kane describes:

> Strange dawn! The morning of the Occident in black Africa was spangled over with smiles, with cannon shots, with shining glass beads. Those who had no history were encountering those who carried the world on their shoulders. It was a morning of accouchement: the known world was enriching itself by a birth that took place in mire and blood.
>
> From shock, the one side made no resistance. They were a people without a past, therefore without memory. The men who were landing on their shores were white, and mad. Nothing like them had ever been known. The deed was accomplished before the people were even conscious of what had happened. (44)

This passage reflects the sudden and horrible manner in which France subdued its Senegalese colony with the pretence of bringing civilization to a land that Europeans have traditionally imagined as being empty and inhabited by barbarians. Some of the consequences of Western colonization of Africa that Césaire inventoried in his *Discourse on Colonialism* (1955) are noticeable in the dilemma that beset the Diallobé community, as the modern schools and administrative establishments of the French colonizers replaced their traditional, educational and political institutions₆. The disaster of colonization is suggested when Samba's father, who is the *Chevalier* [Knight] of the *Diallobé*, meets with Thierno and the Principal of the new French school, in order to discuss whether their society should accept or oppose the educational system of the settlers. On the one hand, the *Diallobé* express their frustration when the French force them to learn French civilization and language. The disappointment is apparent when Thierno worries about the distance that the French school could create between the *Diallobé* and their traditional Coranic school. Thierno asks the School Principal, "What new good are you teaching men's sons, to make them desert our glowing hearths for the benefit of your schools?" (8).

Thierno's fear of the alienation that French education may create in the *Diallobé* community is an implicit criticism of the consequences of colonial politics of assimilation on Africans. As Ihechukwu Madubuike defines it, the concept of assimilation describes "the traditional colonial policy of France" dating back to the days of Richelieu "when the Royal edicts of 1635 and 1642 made native converts of the Catholic faith citizens and natural French men" (*Senegalese* 3). After the French Revolution of 1789, the Ancient Regime survived into a political and cultural assimilation of all the French colonies in Africa. In Senegal, the French initiated assimilation policy as early as the late 19 century. The Article VI of the French Constitution of the Year III states: "The

172

colonies are an integral part of the Republic and are subject to the same law"(3). Assimilation was a primitivistic, condescending, and intrinsically in-egalitarian French policy based on the assumption that the culture, civilization, and institutions of the Africans were inferior to those of the French₇. The civilizationist claim of the French is also apparent in their claim that they were in Africa to bring the light of civilization to a "dark" continent₈. The French's strategy of displacing the local African tradition in order to impose their civilization had negative effects on modern African Francophone societies. From a socio-cultural point of view, this assimilation alienated Africans from their tradition, leaving them in a restless, unsafe, blurring, and indeterminate life where they could identify neither with the tradition of their ancestors nor with the culture of the newcomers. Madubuike observes:

> French education, without a doubt, has produced individuals who are alienated from their traditional culture, who display a Western model of behaviour (they eat at the table, wear suits and ties, spend their holidays in France) but who all the same are not assimilated because they betray by their social conduct some of the traditional values still clinging to their inner selves (167).

The disruption in which assimilation put Africans is visible in *Ambiguous Adventure* in the alienation, restlessness, and confusion that confront Samba during the years of his education in France where the *Diallobé* had sent him to learn how to link wood to wood to built stronger houses (10). While they hoped that the West would teach Samba its philosophy, science and technology, the *Diallobé* dreaded that it would educate him in the "art of winning without being right" (122). Before crossing the Atlantic Ocean to go to Paris and learn western knowledge, Samba already knew that the French school would alienate him from his tradition by ending his priceless education at Thierno's Coranic school and weakening his spiritual ties to the past. When the knight receives a letter from the Chief of the *Diallobé* telling him that the family has decided to send his son to him "so that he might be enrolled in the new [French] school," Samba feels a striking panic in both his father's face and his. After the knight finished reading the letter, he went to bed and started meditating over the ambiguous life that his people would have if they decided to go the French school. Looking at his father's face, Samba could sense anguish and outburst in the Knight's mind. A silent and restless voice in his father's mind told Samba that education might bring irreparable loss and uncertain gain in the *Diallobé* community. On the one hand, the voice tells Samba that the French school would sever the *Diallobé* "from the Glowing Hearth" of the Coranic school (65). On the other hand, the voice confides to Samba that the school would lead the *Diallobé* to a new world where spiritual development would be less valued than economic progress. Kane writes:

What the knight felt when he received the letter was like a blow in his heart. So, the victory of the foreigners was complete! Here were the Diallobe, here was his own family, on their knees before a burst of fireworks. A solar burst, it is true, the midday burst of an exasperated civilization. The knight was suffering deeply in the face of this irreparable thing which was being accomplished here, before his eyes, upon his own flesh. Those who, even down to his own family, who were racing headlong into the future, if they could only understand that their course was a suicide, their sun a mirage! If only he himself were of the stature to rise up before them on the road, and put an end to that blind contest! (63)

The Knight's statement raises questions about the significance of a colonial policy of modernization of Africa in which overindulgence in material gain and spiritual void will compromise the salvation of Africans. The Knight's strongest fear is that "the balance of man" and "the love of God" upon which social and economic stability depend may not be valued in the rush to modernization (63). The Knight perceives modernization as a race in which colonial policy of unequal distribution of resources will turn the *Diallobé* into dependents of the West by jeopardizing their balance of power and social stability. The main goal of the colonists was to subordinate Africans by exploiting their natural resources systematically. As Keith L. Walker argues, in Africa, colonization was a system of exclusive exploitation of all the natural resources of Africans "as well as the exclusive monopoly of the colonial marketplace" (104). This system "not only formally and legally outlawed all direct trade among the colonies or with foreign powers, but also limited local rates and levels of production" (104). The colonizer's exploitation of Africa's natural resources had irreparable consequences on the economic structures of contemporary African societies. This exploitation accounts for the drastic poverty and lack of manufactures in the continent. It created an unequal system of power relations between Europeans and Africans, forcing the latter to rush headlong to Western ideals and policies that do nothing but increase corruption and greed in the continent. The Knight observes:

Happiness is not a function of the mass of responses, but of their distribution. There must be a balance. But the West is possessed by its own compulsion, and the world is becoming westernized. Far from men's resisting the madness of the West at the time when they ought to do so, in order to pick and choose, assimilate or reject, we see them, on the contrary, in all latitudes, a- quiver with covetousness, then metamorphosing themselves in the space of a generation, under the action of this new egotism which the West is scattering abroad. (64)

The Knight's statement suggests the economic and social disruption that neo-colonization can create in Africa by influencing Africa's political elite to participate in the oppression of their nations, at the detriment of the people who had sent them to school. Many African intellectuals returned home only to reject their traditions and impose Western policies and ideals that they were supposed to understand and evaluate before implementing them in their newly independent nations. In this sense, most of the Socialist and Capitalist ideologies that the African political elite implemented in their independent nations in the 1960s and 70s turned out to be instruments of either Western colonial tyranny and totalitarianism or of Western neo-colonial exploitation in the continent. As Frantz Fanon points out, in a post-colonial world "The national bourgeoisie steps into the shoes of the former European settlement" (124) and establishes a mono-party system which is "the modern form of the dictatorship of the bourgeoisie, unmasked, unpainted, unscrupulous, and cynical" (*The Wretched* 133). Indeed, the national bourgeoisie and expatriate intellectuals of newly independent Africa have often been instruments of Western oppression against their own people. The West has often turned these leaders into puppets of European diplomacy and required that they implement in their countries incoherent political and economic systems that served no practical purpose other than to maintain the power that the former colonists gave them9.

Another legacy of colonialism in Africa is the insecurity of African intellectuals when they realize that modernization has alienated them from their tradition. This entrapment of the modern African intellectual is visible when Samba goes to Paris to study philosophy. Walking in the streets of Paris, Samba is overwhelmed by a confluence of material substance and spiritual emptiness around him. Kane writes: " 'These streets are bare,' he was noticing. ' No, they are not empty. One meets objects of flesh in them, as well as objects of metal. Apart from that, they are empty. Ah! One also encounters events. Their succession congests time, as the objects congest the street. Time is obstructed by their mechanic jumble"(119). In Paris, Samba experiences the pain of being invisible to the Western eye. This strange sense of being invisible to Europeans is strongly felt when Pierre-Louis, an African-Martiniquan revolutionary expatriate that Samba meets in Paris, tells Samba:

> Ha, ha, ha! I know what it is. It is not the material absence of your native soil that keeps you in a state of suspended animation, it is its spiritual absence. The West passes you by, you are ignored, you are useless and that at a time when you yourself can no longer pass by the West. Then you succumb to the complex of the Unloved. You feel that your position is precarious. (130)

This dilemma is the same type of estrangement that confronts the African American, the Caribbean, or the African expatriate in the West. This Afro-Diasporic alienation develops in what Gilroy calls the "contact zones," which are these areas in between cultures and histories where many Black intellectuals such as C.L.R. James, Stuart Hall, Anthony Appiah, and Hazel Carby who crisscross the Atlantic Ocean found themselves in and noted the urgency of "cultural interpositionality" and the end of racial particularism (*Black Atlantic*

6). Fanon described this area as this "zone of nonbeing, an extraordinary sterile and arid region, an utterly naked declivity where an authentic upheaval can be born" (*Black Skin* 10). Strange as it is, this alienating "zone" in the West, where the modern Black individual realizes the indeterminacy and instability of his (or her) self, is the same "area" where Samba discovers a way out of his predicament. The same ambiguous position in which Samba finds himself in the West provides him with alternatives to the uprootedness and estrangement in which colonization had put him.

Historically, the detrimental impact of colonization on Africa was also visible on the huge disparity in socio-economic conditions that existed between those who lived in the village and those who were in urban centres. In Senegal, Beginning in the first half of the twentieth century, colonization created a huge gap between wealthy administrative officials called "*citoyens*" [citizens] and the poor inhabitants labelled as "*sujets*"[subjects]. However, the most striking contrast was the disparity that existed in the facilities and living conditions in urban and rural areas. Boahen explains: "In the social field, hospitals were built, though they were found mainly in the urban centres to serve the expatriate communities. Other amenities such as piped water, electricity, dispensaries, paved streets, and the like were also provided, but mainly in the urban centres" (59). Another disparity was the low number of schools in the village in contrast with the comparatively high number of educational centres in the urban centre. This gap in educational opportunity created social inequalities that have certainly contributed to the national divisions that one find today in Africa. It was from an awareness of this disruption -that the French colonial administration and economy created in West

Africa-, that Kane wrote *Ambiguous Adventure* in order to suggest that Africans create a balance between "man" and "work," and between spiritual growth and material expansion. Madubuike explains: "What Kane is arguing for is the reconciliation of the material and the spiritual . . . modernization must not overlook the spiritual concerns of man because these concerns are real" (32-33).

Seeking a balance between tradition and modernity, Kane envisions a world in which Blacks can appropriate Western culture to support their hybrid social, economic, and cultural existence, knowledge, and skills without loosing the spiritual foundation of their African tradition. Kane strongly encourages Africans to enter the doors of Western civilization in search of a magic that can guarantee Africa's survival in the modern world. Yet he urges them not to let modernity replace the traditions of their ancestors. In reaction to the Teacher's claim that by allowing their children to attend the French school, the *Diallobé* will offend God and provoke his anger, Samba's father points out that European education can be appropriated and transformed into tools that will help protect the spiritual and material interests of the *Diallobé*. The dialogue between the teacher and Samba's father speaks to this effect:

> Master, what you say is terrible. May God's pity be upon us . . . But must we push our children into their schools?"
> "It is certain that their school is the better teacher of how to join wood to wood, and that men should learn how to construct dwelling houses that resist the weather."
> "Even at the price of His Sacrifice?"
> "I know also that He must be saved. We must build solid dwellings for men, and within those dwellings we must save God. That I know. But do not ask me what should be done tomorrow morning, for that I do not know." (10)

The Knight's response to Thierno's questions is an objective assessment of the positive impact that Western education could have on the *Diallobé* when it is constructively acquired and utilized. The Knight's idea that French education will help the *Diallobé* maintain their religion and achieve secular development while shaping their future is a realistic acknowledgement of the unpredictable power and hybrid conditions that European culture could create in Africa. The knight's conviction that crossing out into the Western world will help the *Diallobé* develop the knowledge that is necessary for their survival in the modern world reflects his pragmatic and practical approach to economic urgencies. Likewise, the knight's belief that going to school will help the *Diallobé* learn new skills such as the art of building more resistant "dwellings" where they can worship God is a constructive domestication of Western knowledge for African development. In this sense, Kane's fascination with French culture reflects his desire to create a synthesis of Western and African culture that is hybrid and estranging, yet which is the road to Africa's freedom and triumph. In his genuine devotion to hybridity, Kane envisions the development of a future *Diallobé* society in which Western science and African wisdom are intertwined to create human progress. As Lilyan Kesteloot observed, Kane's alternative to under-development is "the coexistence of traditional and modern societies" and the integration of "the culture of Descartes and a certain African mysticism" (*Black Writers* 351).

Yet it is with shock that Samba realizes that Western culture is a fantasy in its claim for an international humanism that is undercut by pervasive ethnocentrism. David Leeming reports an incident in which the French police arrests Baldwin in Marseille on December 1949 for having received a stolen bed sheet that a friend from New York had given him (70). The incident creates in Baldwin the same devastating effect that French ethnocentrism produces in Samba when he realizes that Western cultural and racial ideologies of supremacy were pervasive realities in France, contradicting the ideals of universal liberty, equality, fraternity, and justice of the French. Leeming explains: "For Baldwin this was a terrifying experience. Here in Paris, where he had come to be free, he found himself facing policemen who were 'no better or worse than their American counterparts' " (71). 11

In *Ambiguous Adventure,* Samba is as disillusioned about Paris as Baldwin was at one time. Like Baldwin, Samba realizes that the idea of cosmopolitanism that is easily credited to the French was a façade since the French did not integrate Black culture genuinely into their lives and cultures. Like Baldwin, Samba also finds that the French perceive Africans as inferior people. This racism and primitivism was the result of the obsession that the West has for substance and illusion at the expense of spirituality and truth. Substance, the teacher had told Samba, results in spiritual emptiness. The teacher asked the *Diallobé:* "How are the Diallobe to be given knowledge of the arts and the use of arms, the possession of riches and the wealth of the body, without at the same time weighing them down, dulling their mind" (31). The Chief of the *Diallobé,* who shares the teacher's fear and doubts about the virtues of Western education, says:

> "If I told them [the *Diallobé*] to go to school," he said at last, "they would go en masse. They would learn all the ways of joining wood to wood which we do not know. But, learning, they would also forget. Would what they would learn be worth as much as what they would forget? I should like to ask you: can one learn this without forgetting that, and is what one learns worth what one forgets? (30-31)

181

The biggest tragedy that Samba faces after his return home is the impossibility to reconnect with African tradition without, a priori, paying the price of such atonement. Back home, Samba realizes that becoming who he was required him to strip himself of his Western self, which is feasible upon the condition that he ceases to exist. As Jacques Nantet argues, the only way Samba can reconnect with tradition is to commit "genocide of the souls" (1-2).

The tragic nature of this fate is what leads Samba to refuse to pray, not because he does not wish to do so, but because resistance is the only way for him to surrender to God. Samba meditates: "To constrain God. . . To give Him the choice, between His return within your heart and your death, in the name of His glory . . . He cannot evade the choice, If I constrain Him truly, from the bottom of my heart, will all I have of sincerity" (162). These words seal Samba's fate. Kane writes: "As he [Samba] spoke the fool had begun to walk along behind Samba, burrowing feverishly into the depth of his frock- throat"(162). The fatal end of Samba's life is described in the following scene:

> The fool was in front of him.
> "Promise me that you will pray tomorrow." "NoI do not agree. . . ."
> Without noticing, he had spoken these words aloud. It was then that the fool drew his weapon, and suddenlyeverything went black around Samba Diallo. (162)

The tragic death that Samba experiences in order to be reconnected with his authentic Black culture is similar to the spiritual vacuum that African expatriates who return home, after long years abroad, face before they can regain their sense of self. Reclaiming the African past often requires a tragic spiritual rebirth similar to that of Samba. This is a spiritual rite of passage and a descent into an apocalyptic world in which one lost soul regains a true sense of the past and identity. Samba then is a modern African who surrenders to the unshakeable force of his Black culture before he can regain true consciousness in another world free of the burden of material substance. As critic Kenneth Harrow points out, "his [Samba's] death, far from implying the defeat of the Diallobé society Islamic doctrine, vindicates its view of the ephemerality of mortal existence and the primacy of the spiritual" (169).

Ambiguous Adventure represents the oppression and transformation that colonization brought about in the lives and cultures of modern Africans. As the book suggests, colonization took away the freedom and economic stability of Africans, forcing them to work for the benefit of Western progress. Moreover, *Ambiguous Adventure* provides alternatives to Gilroy's dismissal of Africa's contributions to the formation of Black modernity. Rather than simply dismissing cultural essentialism as being gregarious and backward, as Gilroy has done in *The Black Atlantic,* Kane represents modern Black cultures as being authentic (and hybrid) and nationalist (and internationalist) at the same time. Recognizing such complexity of Black cultures will help us better understand the cultural, economic, and political relationships between Blacks of Africa and of the Diaspora. Moreover, acknowledging such ambiguity will allow us to validate and represent the contribution that African intellectuals have made in the theorizing of Black modernity in Africa and abroad.

Review

Flying Tortoise (Fiction)

Anezi Okoro, *Flying Tortoise* Enugu: Delta Publications 2004

IN twenty-six chapters, Anezi Okoro's *Flying Tortoise* makes a fictional recreation of the tortoise legends. For the first time Tortoise leaves his terrestrial habitat to traverse outer space on a 'discovery mission. In this book the tortoise of Ibo folk tales is transformed into science-oriented tortoise that is equipped with high technology apparati and super-scientific-mathematical mind. But more interesting is that this scientific-minded, science-oriented Tortoise still retains his traditional wisdom, unquenchable optimism, and knowledge all added to his legendary zeal of tackling and confronting obstacles headlong.

The story touches upon modern environmental problems. Tortoise's space probe is sparked by his apparent revulsion on human exploitation of the earth and environment. He watches with horror as a gigantic *Iroko* is brought down by a sawing machine. Even more pathetic is the plight of ants, lizards and other smaller creatures who live in this tree. The impunity with which the flora and fauna of his homeland are devastated sparks off a protest which is underscored by his 'abandoning' earth for outer space. He explores space for life-alternatives in the hope of bringing over his wife, children and other animals there if successful.To his chagrin Tortoise discovers that man has already invaded space with several satellites, probes and other exploration gadgets that litter space. Again he laments man's tardiness even in space. His adventure takes him through all the known planets. He comes back with the knowledge that outer space is not ready yet to support other life forms. But his temporary departure had created a furore as humans had monitored his progress through their space tracking gadgets. He returns to earth a hero. He reels out difficult puzzles for humans to decipher. The idea, apparently, is to force them to recognise that animals have as much intelligence as humans. A sub plot develops around the theme of ethnic jealousies and rivalry which become more apparent as Tortoise's popularity grows.

Meanwhile some other animals interpret this fame as a threat to their own peaceful existence in the forests and they fear that tortoise, proud of his achievements, may begin to harbour ideas about dominating the affairs of the animal kingdom. As this disenchantment grows, divisions increase among them. The bigger animals are the most jealous. Finally, the animals organise themselves into two warring groups and fight a poorly matched war in which the smaller animals: the lizards, snails, serpents, ants, and lightning defeat the bigger ones: Tigers, Elephants, mongooses, hares, leopards, eagles, ducks, etc. It is significant in mediation and conflict resolution efforts that the smaller animals employ their wit and cunning, rather than mere brute force, to defeat their larger opponents.

There may be the temptation to dismiss *Flying Tortoise* as a work of juvenile literature, especially with the tortoise character, yet when considered from the perspective literature that makes an important statement on man and society, the book thrives as a fine study on human nature. It becomes a parable of human folly, jealousy, avarice, ambition and all such positive (or negative) emotions that propel man either to his success or doom. Furthermore, the book dramatizes Fanon's observations on the psychology of the oppressed. The animals make misleading assumptions and conclusions as to the cause(s) of their problems. They blame their own kind and seek the means of eliminating all but the real enemy. It takes a decisive confrontation, however, for them to identify their central adversary:

> Do we need another intervention from lightning to make us accept … that we all belong to the animal kingdom. That our enemy cannot come from your side, nor your enemy from our side. That our true enemy… is man, not Super Tortoise. (174)

This awareness unites the animals as they plan a reception for Super Tortoise. The occasion provides them with the first opportunity to fight man on his own level by using their intelligence. The animals organise several puzzles through which they intend to reveal to man that they want to be treated with respect. Notwithstanding that the scientific language exposing the reader to a plethora of registers makes *Flying Tortoise* a turgid read, the employment of folk story tradition in modern literary narrative is a commendable attempt to preserve oral traditions and cultural heritage.

The Closest of Strangers (Anthology)

Judith Lutge Coullie (Ed.) *The Closest of Strangers: South African Women's Writing*. Johannesburg: Witts University Press 2004

JUDITH Coullie's *The Closest of Strangers* attempts to portray the intricate relationships that lend meaning to the term "existence" and "womanhood" in South Africa. In her statement of objective for her book Coullie acknowledges the essence of all attempts at the great works:

> My hope is that these extracts may teach us how to transcend our own narrow concerns and engage with experiences and truths that may differ from our own, even though such imaginative engagement can only be partial, fragmentary and crude. (3)

The book is divided into nine sections, with each section spanning 9-10 years of history. The book's merit lies in its concentration on stories that denote the 'human angle' to South Africa's frightful history of apartheid and violence. It yields to us the travails of women during the turmoil and turbulence that South Africa had passed through. That the stories and poems are culled from actual biographies, autobiographies and interviews gives the impression of participation on the part of the reader. One feels that he/she is getting the story directly from the narrator. It lends an aura of truth to these experiences.

From that perspective too, the Izibongo(s) (personal/oral praises panegyrics) appear to be appropriately situated within the context of the work. With regard to South Africa's history and its implication for the citizens, historian Cherryl Walker notes:

> [W]omen's sense of community with other women, the basis of their perception of themselves ... was circumscribed by sturdy boundaries of language, ethnicity and the broader race consciousness around which South African society was organized. (*Strangers* 1)

Most of the stories (save few) tend to justify this assertion. In this regard, the stories appear to reflect the "... paradox of ubiquitous racism ... (which has) branded all South Africans, in a sense binding them together in their experiences ... of the extremes of segregation"(3).

Although it might appear a bit hasty to conclude that the story of South Africa is that of violence, yet each of the nine sections in this anthology reveals the vicious strings that run through the whole South African debacle. From wars, lynching, mob killings, incarceration, police molestation and forced evictions, to rape, thefts, escapes, forced labour, spurned or thwarted love and family separations, the lives of South African women chronicle two centuries of violence. Projecting from the consciousness of the victims or 'victim witnesses', the nightmarish tales adjust the lens of reality to reveal the universal humanity beneath the events. I believe that this is one of the editorial objectives of this compilation.

The first section of the book is entitled "The Birth of South Africa." Stories in this section detail the bloodbath that preceded the birth of South Africa from the Anglo-Boer wars. Sarah Raal's story chronicles her account of the many dangers she faced fighting alongside men in the war. The general picture conveyed is that the women suffered and were exposed to even greater dangers than their men during the wars.

"Unions and Divisions" contains four stories out of which only one (Prue Smith's) appears to have relevance to the underlying theme of British racism after the Anglo-Boer wars. Racial discrimination was meted out to non-British nationals including the Dutch. Although this section is preceded by a good introduction, the stories that appear here do not lend it much structural cohesion. Perhaps more stories directly concerned with the basic expositions of the introduction should have featured here to achieve the unity of vision. Prue Smith's account might be seen as a white woman's reaction to entrenched racial segregation. In contrast, she forges emotional alliance with her black nurse upon whom she had depended. Although the story comes to us from Smith's white viewpoint, yet her revelation that the maid's baby was named after her seems to underscore the mutual emotional dependence of two human beings irrespective of the divisions of the society. Mgqwetho's Izibongo in this section has very little relevance with the objective. Perhaps its inclusion is simply justified by the period of its production.

"Enfranchisement and Disenfranchisement," chronicles events that happened between 1930 and 1940. This was the period of great political upheaval especially for blacks and Asians singled for racist victimisations around this period. Then, the main opposing political party, the Communist Party, enjoyed much popularity. It was a period of great trial for this party as its tenets and practices were put to severe test. One of such tests is that of the relationships between different racial groups. This is illustrated in Pauline Podbrey's story of the love between herself and her Indian husband. That this story appears in "Foundations of Apartheid' seems to render the structural divisions unnecessary. Indeed but for some few

190

cases, many of the stories would have conveniently appeared as one major section. For instance the stories in "Enfranchisement" and "Foundations of Apartheid" could have conveniently featured as one section with "Apartheid Escalates" or "Winds of Repression."

However, with the preoccupation with 'violence' in the stories, there still appear some ideas of positive dimensions. While Dr Goonam's experience in "Enfranchisement..." captures prevalent gender prejudices, dichotomies and challenges, Katie Makanya's account of her job experience with Dr McCord reveals like Prue Smith, that love, loyalty and dedication transcend the racial boundary. In this guise, Charlene Smith's story of rape, and even more importantly, her 'liberated' awareness which guides her report of the incidence, reveal a quality of awareness that attempts to transcend the confines of environment. Her report admits of success in overcoming racial biases which seem to dictate and muddle our perception of reality. It is significant that her report details a cognisance that insight that although raped by a black man, there lies a deeper understanding of the human nature that drives our predictable reactions:

> I cry, "I'm terribly sorry, but he raped me. I don't have my clothes with me".
> My white neighbour goes to fetch his wife. My black neighbour leads me gently away.
> "Please cut off this masking tape. I can't move properly." I try to move my bloodied hand. My black neighbour gets something and with the greatest gentleness cuts off the masking tape and frees my hand. (368)

After this report she observes:

I tell you the race of my neighbours because I want you to know that rape is not about race, as some South Africans think. It is not about what men do. It is about what a few sick individuals do. It has nothing to do with race or malehood. Indeed, for most part men treated me better than women that night. (368)

Smith's traumatic experience, reported in "The New South Africa" nearly deadens the ironical twist of the tale but for her exceptional depth of awareness. Such level of consciousness would readily lend an insight to forging the dream of the new South Africa. Her message of hope seems to proclaim that people need to cross gender and racial boundaries in order to develop the human potential. Smith's report appears to highlight the view that life and existence in the new South Africa can only be achieved when people have a greater understanding of their neighbours (work, home, community) some of whom had been their closest strangers in the past. One way of achieving this insight appears to be the objective of this anthology. With decades of political, cultural and economic divide officially dismantled in South Africa, individuals are challenged to eschew emotional and psychological attitudes by availing themselves of the opportunity being offered to synergise others' experiences.

It must be observed that the "Izibongo" oral poems do not communicate much of message or art. Their scant yield in meaning and poetic virtuosity may be attributed to the brevity of their presentation. Also, some of the stories coming as autobiographies have the ring of contrivance. A good example is Winnie Mandela's account of her early relationship with her husband constructed to suit some simply emotional or post traumatic purpose. Judith Coullie's anthology could however be enriched with the experiences of black women in subsequent editions.

End of Unheard Narratives (Critical Perspectives)

Bettina Weiss (Ed.), *The End of Unheard Narratives: Contemporary Perspectives on Southern African Literature*, Heidelberg: Kalliope 2004

IN her introduction to *The End of Unheard Narratives* Bettina Weiss puts forward the proposition that the title signifies that 'former(ly) unheard narratives' have 'receive(d) a powerful expression' and have by the book publication 'cease(d) to remain in the closet.' The intent on giving voice to the 'marginal' or minority voices achieves the congenial purpose of reappraising the philosophical and socio political imperatives which give impetus to 'silencing narratives' deemed 'unpleasant' or even 'dangerous.'

The book diligently identifies such narratives as those dwelling on themes of homosexuality, HIV/AIDS, prostitution and sexual exploitation, and all the stigmatised peoples of these categories 'who struggle for acceptance and humanity.' Consequently the essays are commendable for their promise of giving 'an enlarged and enlightening insight' although the major entries become, for the first and second parts, a consolidation of fringe and 'abject' subject matters replete with their complex intrigues and oppositions all plodding vicariously along the familiar path of gender and social conflicts inscribed by the feminist movement that has blown from across Europe and through the rest of the western world.

Annemarie van Niekerk's 'A Leaking Categories' featuring an autobiographical work *Rachel, Woman of the Night* by a South African sex worker Rachael Lindsay who

193

explores the inside prism of 'the oldest trade in the world' makes a befitting introduction to the hardy objective of authenticating the 'Other' particularly as the subject of prostitution had hitherto been neglected in major literary materials of the bio- and auto-biographical kinds. Niekerk's highlight of the entry of South African literature to the discourse on topic of prostitution is treated with notable objectivity and scholarship which seeks to identify with the protagonist's point of view and to commend neither censure nor opprobrium. This capacity for objectification of the literary material in critical studies as against intensely opinionated and dominantly theoretical prejudice is a much needed approach to African literature particularly with the fad of 'talking back' and 'writing back' which has engaged many a theorist of postcolonial literatures, and which, in Berveley Dube's review 'Re-Imagining the Prostitute in Society: A Critique of the Male Writer's Perspective in Zimbabwean Literature,' shows a pattern where early prejudices against minority opinions seem to be giving way to a less subjective, more sympathetic attitude on the part of writers of fiction.

Lizzy Attree's paper 'Reshaping Communities: The Representation of HIV/AIDS in Literature from South Africa and Zimbabwe' surveys different perspectives on the AIDS pandemic that has ravaged Southern African nations, dutifully ferreting out attempts at the re-inscriptions of Africa as a dark continent with the spread and devastation (not excluding the myths and ignorance surrounding it) of the disease that has ravaged exploited and poverty stricken African communities. However, the study ignores to present indigenous alternatives to modern transitions in the post colonial history of Africa's exploitation, an indication of the extent of the amnesia of modern Southern African academics about the overarching importance of the indigenous heritage, and thereby of history beyond apartheid and postcoloniality. The result is that the new South African amalgam of racial attitudes in the region might have formulated another typecast of sorts bordering on the main-other, persecutor-victim divide which is not mitigated by the shallow blaming of 'homophobic attitudes' and patriarchal power relations' for the silencing of some of the world's 'minority' sexual expressions today.

Part II 'Voicing Tough Facts and Gentle Suggestions' appears a redundant sectionalising of clearly homogenous materials as the two remarkable works of Tom Odhiambo: 'Socio Sexual Experiences of Black South African Men' and Bettina Weiss: 'Approach to Homoerotic Female Desire' may well have functioned in 'Abject Bodies.' This may also apply to Robert Mupond's 'The Eyes of a Buck: Fighting the Child in Zimbabwean Short Story in English' editorially figured in 'tough facts/ gentle suggestions' for the writer's treatment of the child figure in literature, an approach that reexamines held assumptions which the writer confronts at the beginning of his essay i.e., of children being in Leslie Fiedler's words 'symbols of offended innocence' especially in the creative writings of 'frontline' nation states as has been the histories of the Southern (and other) African nations.

Three papers by Katrin Berndt ('Eloquent Silence as a Mode of Identity'), Margie Orford ('Transition, Trauma and Triumph: Contemporary Namibian Women's Literature') and the duo of Dorothy Driver and Meg Samuelson ('History's Intimate Visions: Yvonne Vera's *The Stone Virgins*') form the third part of the book tagged Re(N)egotiating and Restoring Identities. Of these three, Katrin Berndt's 'Eloquent Silence' takes the arguable position that the silence of the female protagonist can be 'eloquent' and (for Berndt) provides an opening ('interstice') for expressing so called 'subaltern approaches' for truthfulness as against the lies of official historiographies on Southern African movement and progress. Yet there is something ultimately distasteful, for its racist assumptions, of Berndt's idea (unabashedly Spivak's) of the 'lack of expressive and narrative power of inferior group.' The author's argument deliberately replete with infestations of superficial post colonial theories of 'subjective' and 'objective' approaches to truthfulness reinforces outmoded hegemonic myths and fallacies. It appropriates to itself the same language and definitions of untoward inscriptions which function to the detriment of the victims of colonialism's entrenched interests such as the Southern Africa of their study.

These give the perspectives coming from *The End of Unheard Narratives* a tendency to further recast the alienation of those 'abject' conditions and not their integration in serious literary or philosophical preoccupation. Here again one wonders at the editor's position that 'prostitutes and women voices were/are silenced...for the purposes of 'creating controversial moral values,' especially where the main historical conveyors of these morality and attitudes have been Western /Hebraic-Christian civilisation and its dubious theories of world history, human existence, racial, family or sex relations –the last of which Southern African literatures have lately been identified as 'individualising' or particularising upon. This important historical insight is lost on the contributors, excepting Odhiambo -who mentions only partially- that 'Christianity emphasised heterosexuality and condemned homoerotic practices,' thereby adding to the relevant observation that the redoubtable legacies of the west lie behind the world's most noxious sickness of bigotry, conquest and domination of the perceived other. Yet Odhiambo in his paper asserts rather lamely that 'many

African societies have had alternate sex practices for ages' without evident basis for that claim. Similarly Bettina Weiss declares that 'this so-called un-Africanness (of lesbianism and homosexuality) was/is not that un-African at all (119) all in gallant efforts to subvert the anti-homoerotic rhetoric. This is where the idea of contextual/literary frameworks of artistic interpretations clogs observations on the larger merits of creative works. It marks an academic tendency to stultify literature with a stricture complex in which many a generation of critical studies can be trapped for longer, deficient periods of the rest of its history.

One is however optimistic that, with the end of apartheid and the so-called political literature produced by its mixed black, white, and coloured populace, all that the new 'individual' themes have to offer are not entirely riveted on counteracting or propagating fringe subject matters which the first through the third parts of this study have done. Thus the last part, 'The Past a Mediator for the Present' marks the important stirrings of perception in Southern African literature as Agnes Murungi's 'The Invention of (Oral) Tradition and the Imagining of a New Nation' shows of Ellen Kuzwayi's *Sit Down and Listen* collection of short stories. Murungi harmonises the notion of tradition and modernity as separate concepts. Her idea of a 'useable past,' drawing a relevant note from the cerebral Lewis Nkosi whose interactions with other African writers of his times highlight this effort, serves, in Murungi's excellent phrase, 'to recognise a South African identity that is based on a deeper sense of cultural retrieval.'

This negotiation of a tenuous trado-modern divide witnesses a wider experimentation with the form and style of narrative involving established and popular traditions of black (and other non-black) culture(s). Agnes Murungi's study and Jessica Henry's "'How All Life Is Lived in Patches":

Quilting Metaphors in the Fiction of Yvonne Vera' are therefore the watershed in these contemporary perspectives on Southern African literary aesthetics mainly for their departure from the preoccupation with aesthetically stymied symptoms of adolescent psychosis, sex/ gender violence replete in the celebrated literatures of the Southern African region.

As a work which in the editor's promise 'hold(s) the potential to subvert and destabilise rigid conceptions' this objective, it must be conceded, has been swiftly and effectively executed with just twelve critical submissions for which editor Weiss is to be commended and encouraged. It is a step in the right direction as it contributes eloquently to the discourse towards the elimination of all manners of prejudice, violence and discrimination that have tainted the human race through its slow, tortuous civilisations. But sustaining of this burden of self and collective redemption from past and present entrapments certainly involves concentrated, deeper, and more original insights on the part of Southern African scholars and writers.

Notes and Bibliography

Chapter One
Dialogue and Transition in Recent Oeuvres

Notes
[1]In its introduction, it is stated that Gamji College 'is the same tragedy of misplaced values, directionlessness and exhibition of political charisma bred on the stable of ethnic chauvinism that we have seen in Children of Koloko.'
[2]In The Trouble with Nigeria Chinua Achebe states mater-of-factly that 'the trouble with Nigeria is simply and squarely' a failure of leadership, a point which Chin Ce corroborates in entirety in "Bards and Tyrants" (ALJ B5 2005).

Works Cited

Ce, Chin. An African Eclipse and other Poems. Enugu: Handel Books 2000
— --- --- . Children of Koloko. Enugu: Handel Books 2001
— — --- . The Visitor. Lagos: Handel Books 2005
— --- --- . Gamji College. Enugu: Handel Books 2002
Delores, Vine Jnr. God Is Red: A Native View of Religion. Colorado: Fulcrum Publishing 1994
Lawrence, D. H. Sons and Lovers. London: Penguin 1963
The Tragedies of Shakespeare and Achebe

Chapter Two
The Tragedies of Shakespeare and Achebe

Note
1The deaths of Cordelia and Ophelia in King Lear and Hamlet respectively should not be taken as a denial of justice. The deaths of these two innocent characters could be seen as a demonstration of the pervasive influence of evil; what triumphs at the end of both stories is virtue and not vice.

Works Cited

Achebe, Chinua. Arrow of God. London : Heinemann, 1974
— — —. Things Fall Apart. London: Heinemann, 1958

Arthos, John. Shakespeare's use of Dream and Vision. London: Bowes and Bowes, 1977.

Bradley, A.C. Shakespearean Tragedy. London: Macmillan, 1904

Bratchell, D.F. ed. Shakespearean Tragedy. London: Routledge, 1990.

Campbell, Lily B. Shakespeare's Tragic Heroes. London: Methuen, 1961

Ejizu, Christopher. Ofo: Igbo Ritual Symbol. Enugu: Fourth Dimension Publishers, 1986

Mehl, Dieter. Shakespeare's Tragedies. Cambridge: CUP, 1986

Ogbaa, Kalu. Gods, Oracles and Divinations. New Jersey: Africa World Press, Inc., 1992

Opie, Iona and Moira Tatem. A Dictionary of Superstitions. Oxford: OUP, 1989

Shakespeare, William. Julius Caesar. Singapore: Longman, 1959

— — —. King Lear. London: Longman, 1974

— — —. Hamlet. London: Longman, 1968

— — —. Macbeth. Singapore : Longman, 1960

Turner, Harold. Living Tribal Religions. London: Ward Lock Educational, 1971

Chapter Three
New Male Characters

Note

1.We use the word (Neo)colonial as it is written to refer to the colonial and neo- colonial era and/or figure. When we use colonial by itself, we are referring to the colonial era and figure and when weI use neo-colonial, we are referring to the post-independence era. Thus, (neo)colonial, again, refers to the simultaneous discussion of both the colonial and neo-colonial era or figure.

Works Cited

Aidoo, Ama Ata. Anowa. London: Longman, 1970.

- - -. Our Sister Killjoy or Reflections from a Black-Eyed Squint. London: Drumbeat, 1981.

- - -. "Ghana: To Be a Woman." Sisterhood is Global. Ed. Robin Morgan. New York: Anchor Press, 1984.

- - -. Dilemma of A Ghost. London: Longman, 1965.

- - -. Changes: A Love Story. New York: The Feminist Press, 1991

Amadiume, Ifi. Male Daughters, Female Husbands. New Jersey: Zed Books Ltd., 1987.

Boyce Davies, Carole. Black Women, Writing and Identity. Migrations of the Subject. New York: Routledge, 1994.

Brown, Lloyd. Women Writers in Black Africa. London: Greenwood Press, 1981.

Caminero-Santangelo, Byron. "Neo-colonialism and the Betrayal Plot in A Grain of Wheat: Ngugi wa Thiong'o's Re-Vision of Under Western Eyes." Research in African Literatures 29.1 (Spring 1998): 139-52.

Cesaire, Aime. Discourse on Colonialism. New York: Monthly Review Press, 1972.

Du Bois, W. E. B. The Souls of Black Folk. New York: Signet, 1995.

Fanon, Frantz. Black Skin, White Masks. New York: Grove Press, Inc., 1967.

- - -.The Wretched of the Earth. New York: Grove Weidenfeld, 1963.

Chapter Four
Marriage and Fatherhood Stories

Works Cited

Adams, Michele, and Scott Coltrane. "Boys and Men in Families: The Domestic Production of Gender, Power, and Privileges." Handbook of Studies on Men & Masculinities. Ed. Michael Kimmel, Jeff Hearn, and R. W. Connell. London: Sage Publications, 2004. 230-248.

Amato, Paul R. "More than Money? Men's Contributions to their Children's Lives" Men in Families: When do they get Involved? What Difference does it make? Eds. Allan Booth & Ann C. Crouter. Mahwah NJ: Lawrence Erlbaum Associates, 1998.

Assimeng, Max. Social Structure of Ghana: A Study in Persistence and Change. Tema: Ghana Publishing Corporation, 1981.

Coltrane, Scott. "Farming" Men and Masculinities: A Social, Cultural, and Historical Encyclopaedia. Eds. Kimmel, Michael & Amy Aronson. Santa Barbara: ABC-CLIO, 2004. 272-274.

Connell, Robert W. The Men and the Boys. Berkeley: University of California Press, 2000.

Gilmore, D. David. Manhood in the Making: Cultural Concepts of Masculinity. New Haven: Yale UP, 1990.

Griswold, Robert L. "Fatherhood" American Masculinities: A Historical Encyclopaedia. Ed. Bret E. Carroll Thousand Oaks: Sage Publications, 2003. 161-164.

Gyekye, Kwame. African Cultural Values: An Introduction. Accra: Sankofa Publishing Company, 2003.

Kimmel, Michael & Amy Aronson. Eds. Men and Masculinities: A Social, Cultural and Historical Encyclopaedia. Santa Barbara: ABC-CLIO, 2004.

Lamb, Michael E. "Fatherhood then and Now" Men in Families: When do they get Involved? What Difference does it make? Eds. Allan Booth & Ann C. Crouter. Mahwah NJ: Lawrence Erlbaum Associates, 1998.

Meyer, Birgit. "Ghanaian Popular Cinema and the Magic in and of Film" Magic and Modernity: Interfaces of Revelation and Concealment. Eds. Birgit Meyer and Peter Pels. Stanford: Stanford UP, 2003. 200-222.

Meyer, Birgit. Popular Ghanaian Cinema. Netherlands: WOTRO, 1999.

Morgan, David. "Family, Gender, and Masculinities." The Masculinities Reader. Eds. Whitehead, Stephen M. & Frank Barrett J. Cambridge: Blackwell Publishers, 2001. 223-232.

Nock, Steven L. Marriage in Men's Lives. New York: Oxford University Press,1998.

Nukunya, G.K. Tradition and Change in Ghana: An Introduction to Sociology. Accra: Ghana Universities Press, 1992.

Nukunya, G. K. Kinship and Marriage among the Anlo Ewe. New York: The Athlone Press, 1969.

Rontundo, Anthony E. "Patriarchs and Participants: A Historical Perspective on Fatherhood" Beyond Patriarchy: Essays by Men on Pleasure, Power, and Change. Michael Kaufman Eds. Toronto: Oxford UP, 1987. 64-80.

Sarpong, Peter. Ghana in Retrospect: Some Aspects of Ghanaian Culture. Tema: Ghana Publishing Corporation, 1974.

Stoltenberg, John. Refusing to be a Man: Essays on Sex and Justice. London: UCL Press, 2000.

Wolf, Clark. "Power and Equality in Intimate Relationships" Men and Power. Ed. Kuyupers, A. Joseph Halifax: Fernwood Publishing, 1999. 127-145.

Video Films

A Call at Midnight, (VHS) Video, 119 Minutes, Colour, English; Written: Samuel Nai, Directed: Vero Quashie, Produced: Moro Yaro Accra: Princess Film Productions, 2001.

Dabi Dabi I Video (VHS), 89 Minutes, Colour English & Twi, 2002; Dabi Dabi II Video (VHS), 83 Minutes, Colour, English & Twi, 2002; Dabi Dabi III video (VHS), 79 Minutes, Colour, English & Twi, 2003; all Written: James Aboagye and Edward Frimpong, Directed: Kenny McCauley, Produced: Miracle Films Production, Accra.

Idols of Heart, (VHS) Video, 111 Minutes, Colour, English; Written: Wisdom Setsoafia & Emeka Nwabueze, Directed: E. Dugbartey Nanor & Victor Emeghara, Produced: D'Joh Media Craft & Kama Marketing, Accra: 2001.

Jennifer, Video (VHS), 121 Minutes, Colour, English, Written: Samuel Gaskin, Directed: Nick Narh Teye Produced: E. Teye-Botchway, Accra: 1998. Nightmare, Video (VHS), 88 Minutes, Colour, English; Written: Pastor

Kingsley Obed & Godwin Kotey, Directed: Seth Ashong-Katai, Produced: Morning Star Productions: 2001.

Odasani I Video (VHS), 88 Minutes, Colour, English & Twi; Written: Kwaku Twumasi & James Aboagye, Directed: Samuel Nyamekye Producer: Owusu Sekyere Accra: Rabi Videos, 2003.

Odasani II Video (VHS), 111 Minutes, Colour, English & Twi; Written: Kwaku Twumasi & James Aboagye, Directed: Samuel Nyamekye Produced: Samuel Nyamekye Accra: Rabi Videos, 2003.

A Stab in the Dark I, Video (VHS), 113 Minutes, Colour, English; Written: Sam Nai & Veronica Quashie, Directed: Veronica Quashie, Produced: Princess Film Production, Accra: 1999.

Stolen Bible 1, Video, (VHS), 84 Minutes, Colour, English; Stolen Bible II, Video, (VHS), 99 Minutes, Colour, English; Written, Directed, Produced: Augustine Abbey, Accra: Great Idikoko Ventures, 2001

Time Video (VHS), 100 Minutes, Colour, English; Written: Godwin John/Willy Ajenge, Directed: Ifeanyi Onyeabor, Produced: E. Dugbartey Nanor, Accra: 2000.

Tribal War I. Video (VHS) 99 Minutes, Colour, English, Ewe, & Twi; 2002; Tribal War II (VHS) 113 Minutes, Colour, English, Ewe, & Twi; 2003 both Written, Directed, and Produced: Samuel Nyamekye. Accra: Rabi Videos.

Chapter Five
Postcolonial 'Writing Back'

Works Cited

Achebe, Chinua. "The African Writer and the English Language" in Chinua Achebe's Things Fall Apart: A Casebook. Ed. Isidore Okpewho. Oxford: Oxford UP, 2003. 55-65.

- - -. "An Image of Africa." The Massachusetts Review 18.4 (1977): 782-94.

- - -. Things Fall Apart. 1958. Oxford: New Windmills-Heinemann, 1971.

Adam, Ian and Helen Tiffin, eds. Past the Last Post: Theorizing Post-Colonialism and Post-Modernism. New York: Harvester Wheatsheaf, 1991.

Adams, David. Colonial Odysseys: Empire and Epic in the Modernist Novel. Ithaca: Cornell UP, 2003.

Aegerter, Lindsay Pentolfe. "A Dialectic of Autonomy and Community: Tsitsi Dangarembga's Nervous Conditions." Tulsa Studies in Women's Literature 15.2 (1996): 231-40.

Appiah, Kwame Anthony. In My Father's House: Africa in the Philosophy of Culture. New York: Oxford UP, 1992.

Ashcroft, Bill, Gareth Griffiths and Helen Tiffin. The Empire Writes Back: Theory and practice in post-colonial literatures. 2 ed. London: Routledge, 2002.

Ashcroft, W.D. "Intersecting Marginalities: Post-colonialism and Feminism." Kunapipi 11.2 (1989): 23-35.

Beckham, Jack M. "Achebe's Things Fall Apart." The Explicator 60.4 (2002): 229-231.

Begum, Khani. "Construction of the Female Subject in Postcolonial Literature: Tsitsi Dangarembga's Nervous Conditions." Journal of Commonwealth and Postcolonial Studies 1.1 (1993): 21-27.

Boehmer, Elleke. Colonial and Postcolonial Literature: Migrant Metaphors. New York: Oxford UP, 1995.

Bohlmann, Otto. Conrad's Existentialism. New York: St. Martin's, 1991.

Booker, Keith M. The African Novel in English: An Introduction. Portsmouth: Heinemann, 1998.

Briault-Manus, Vicki. "The Interaction of 'Race' and Gender as Cultural Constructs in Tsitsi Dangarembga's Nervous Conditions." Commonwealth Essays and Studies 26.2 (2003): 23-32.

Carroll, David. Chinua Achebe: Novelist, Poet, Critic. Basingstoke: Macmillan, 1990.

Cobham, Rhonda. "Problems of Gender and History in the Teaching of Things Fall Apart." Chinua Achebe's Things Fall Apart: A Casebook. Ed. Isidore Okpewho. Oxford, Oxford UP, 2003. 165-80.

Dangarembga, Tsitsi. Nervous Conditions. 1988. New York: Seal, 1989.

Darby, Phillip. "Postcolonialism." At the Edge of International Relations: Postcolonialism, Gender and Dependency. London: Pinter, 1997. 12-32.

Davies, Carole Boyce. "Motherhood in the Works of Male and Female Igbo Writers: Achebe, Emecheta, Nwapa and Nzekwu." Ngambika: Studies of Women in African Literature. Ed. C. B. Davies and Anne Adam Graves. Trenton: Africa World, 1986. 241-56.

Dodgson, Pauline. "Coming in From the Margins: Gender in Contemporary Zimbabwean Writing." Post-Colonial Literatures: Expanding the Canon. Ed. Deborah L. Madsen. London: Pluto, 1999. 88-103.

Eagleton, T. Criticism and Ideology: A Study in Marxist Literary Theory. London: Verso, 1976.

Gandhi, Leela. Postcolonial Theory: A Critical Introduction. Sydney: Allen & Unwin, 1998.

Gikandi, Simon. "Chinua Achebe and the Invention of African Culture."Research in African Literatures 32.3 (2001): 3-8.

Harris, Michael. Outsiders & Insiders: Perspectives of Third World Culture in British and Post-Colonial Fiction. New York: Peter Lang, 1992.

Harrow, Kenneth W. Thresholds of Change in African Literature: The Emergence of a Tradition. Portsmouth: Heinemann, 1994.

Hogan, Patrick Colm. "Culture and Despair: Chinua Achebe's Things Fall Apart." Colonialism and Cultural Identity: Crises of Tradition in the Anglophone Literatures of India, Africa and the Carribean. Albany: State U of New York P, 2000. 103-35.

Huggan, Graham. "African literature and the anthropological exotic." The Post-Colonial Exotic: Marketing the Margins. London: Routledge, 2001. 34-57.

Innes, C.L. " A Less Superficial Picture: Things Fall Apart." Chinua Achebe. Cambridge: Cambridge UP, 1990. 21-41.

Jameson, Fredric. "Third-World Literature in the Era of Multinational Capitalism." Social Text 15 (1986): 65-88.

Jeyifo, Biodun. "Okonkwo and His Mother: Things Fall Apart and Issues of Gender in the Constitution of African Postcolonial Discourse." Chinua Achebe's Things Fall Apart: A Casebook. Ed. Isidore Okpewho. Oxford: Oxford UP, 2003. 181-99.

Kalu, Anthonia C. Women, Literature and Development in Africa. Trenton: Africa World , 2001.

Katrak, Ketu H. "Decolonizing Culture: Towards a Theory for Postcolonial Women's Texts." Modern Fiction Studies 35.1 (1989): 157-79.

Kortenaar, Neil Ten. "How the Centre is Made to Hold in Things Fall Apart." Postcolonial Literatures: Achebe, Ngugi, Desai, Walcott. Ed. Michael Parker and Roger Starkey. Basingstoke: Macmillan, 1995. 31-51.

Linton, Patricia. "Ethical Reading and Resistant Texts." Post-Colonial Literatures: Expanding the Canon. Ed. Deborah L. Madsen. London: Pluto, 1999. 29-44.

McClintock, Anne. "The Angel   of Progress: Pitfalls of the term Postcolonialism'." Colonial Discourse/ Postcolonial Theory. ed. Francis Barker, Peter Hulme and Margaret Iversen. Manchester: Manchester UP, 1994. 253-66.

Miller, Christopher. Blank Darkness: Africanist Discourse in French. Chicago: U of Chicago P, 1985.

- - -. "The Discoursing Heart: Conrad's Heart of Darkness." Joseph Conrad: New Casebooks. Ed. Elaine Johnson. Basingstoke: Macmillan, 1996. 87-102.

Nnoromele, Patrick C. "The Plight of a Hero in Achebe's Things Fall Apart." College Literature 27.2 (2000): 146-56.

Nzenza, Sekai. "Women in postcolonial Africa: between African men and Western feminists." At the Edge of International Relations: Postcolonialism, Gender and Dependency. Ed. Phillip Darby. London: Pinter, 1997. 214-35.

Ogungbesan, Kolawole. "Politics and the African Writer." Critical Perspectives on Chinua Achebe. Ed. C.L. Innes and Bernth Lindfors. London: Heinemann, 1979. 37-46.

Okhamafe, Imafedia. "Genealogical Determinism in Things Fall Apart." Genealogy & Literature. Ed. Lee Quinby. Minneapolis: U of Minnesota P, 1995. 134-154.

Osei-Nyame, Kwadwo. "Chinua Achebe Writing Culture: Representations of Gender and Tradition in Things Fall Apart." Research in African Literatures 30.2 (1999): 148-62.

Osei-Nyame, Jnr., Kwadwo. "The 'Nation' between the 'Genders': Tsitsi Dangarembga's Nervous Conditions." Current Writing: Text and Reception in Southern Africa 11.1 (1999): 55-66.

Pelikan Straus, Nina. "The Exclusion of the Intended from Secret Sharing in Conrad's Heart of Darkness." Novel 20.2 (1987): 123-37.

Povey, John. "The Novels of Chinua Achebe." Introduction to Nigerian Literature. Ed. Bruce King. New York: Africana Publishing Corporation, 1972. 97-112.

Quayson, Ato. "Feminism, Postcolonialism and the Contradictory Orders of Modernity." Postcolonialism: Theory, Practice or Process? Cambridge: Polity, 2000. 103-131.

Rowell, Charles H. "An Interview with Chinua Achebe" (1989). Chinua Achebe's Things Fall Apart: A Casebook. Ed. Isidore Okpewho. Oxford, Oxford UP, 2003. 249-272.

Said, Edward. Orientalism. Harmondsworth: Penguin, 1985.

Schwartz, Nina. "The Ideologies of Romanticism in Heart of Darkness." Dead Fathers: The Logic of Transference in Modern Narrative. Ann Arbor: U of Michigan P, 1994. 31-54.

Schwarz, Daniel R. "Signing the Frame, Framing the Sign: Multiculturalism, Canonicity, Pluralism, and the Ethics of Reading Heart of Darkness." Rereading Conrad. Columbia: U of Missouri P, 2001. 35-57.

Skinner, John. The Stepmother Tongue: An Introduction to New Anglophone Fiction.New York: St. Martin's, 1998.

Spivak, Gayatri. "Can the subaltern speak?" (1985). Marxist Interpretations of Culture. Ed. Cary Nelson and Lawrence Grossberg. Basingstoke: Macmillan, 1988. 271-313.

Stratton, Florence. "How Could Things Fall Apart For Whom They Were Not Together?" Contemporary African Literature and the Politics of Gender. London: Routledge, 1994. 22-38.

Strobel, Susanne. "Floating into Heaven or Hell? The river journey in Mary Kingsley's Travels in West Africa and Joseph Conrad's Heart of Darkness." Being/s in Transit: Travelling, Migration, Dislocation. Ed. Liselotte Glage. Amsterdam: Rodopi, 2000. 69-82.

Sugnet, Charles. "Nervous Conditions: Dangarembga's feminist reinvention of Fanon." The Politics of (M)othering: Womanhood, Identity, and

Resistance in African Literature. Ed. Obioma Nnaemeka. London: Routledge, 1997. 33-49.

Suleri, Sara. "Woman Skin Deep: Feminism and the Postcolonial Condition." Contemporary Postcolonial Theory: A Reader. Ed. Padmini Mongia. London: Arnold, 1996. 335-46.

Thieme, John. "Conrad's 'hopeless' binaries: Heart of Darkness and postcolonial interior journeys." Postcolonial Con-Texts: Writing Back to the Canon. London: Continuum, 2001.15-52.

Tiffin, Helen. "Post-Colonial Literatures and Counter-Discourse." Kunapipi 9.3 (1987): 17-34.

Traoré, Ousseynou B. "Why the Snake-Lizard killed his mother: inscribing and decentering "Nneka" in Things Fall Apart." The Politics of (M)othering: Womanhood, Identity, and Resistance in African Literature. Ed. Obioma Nnaemeka. London: Routledge, 1997. 50-68.

Uwakweh, Pauline Ada. "Debunking Patriarchy: The Liberational Quality of Voicing in Tsitsi Dangarembga's Nervous Conditions." Research in African Literatures 26.1 (1995): 75-84.

Veit-Wild, Flora. "'Women Write About the Things that Move Them.' A Conversation with Tsitsi Dangarembga." Moving Beyond Boundaries, Volume 2: Black Women's Diasporas. Ed. Carole Boyce Davies. London: Pluto, 1995. 27-31.

Vizzard, Michelle. "Of Mimicry and Women: Hysteria and Anticolonial Feminism in Tsitsi Dangarembga's Nervous Conditions." SPAN (October 1993): 202-10.

wa Thiong'o, Ngugi. Decolonising the Mind: The Politics of Language in African Literature. London: James Currey, 1986.

Watts, Cedric. "'A Bloody Racist': About Achebe's View of Conrad." Yearbook of English Studies 13 (1983): 196-209.

Wren, Robert M. Achebe's World: The Historical and Cultural Context of the Novels of Chinua Achebe. Essex: Longman, 1981.

Wright, Derek, ed. "Introduction: Writers and Period." Contemporary African Fiction. Bayreuth: Bayreuth U, 1997. 5-15.

Yeats, W.B. "The Second Coming" (1921). The Norton Anthology of Poetry. 4 ed.Ed. Margaret Ferguson, Mary Jo Salter and Jon Stallworthy. New York: Norton, 1996. 1091.

Yegenoglu, Meyda. Colonial fantasies: Towards a feminist reading of Orientalism.Cambridge: Cambridge UP, 1998.

Chapter Six
Identity in a Postcolonial Void

Works Cited
Achebe, Chinua. Things Fall Apart. African Writers Series. Oxford, Eng.: Heinemann, 2000.

Adejumobi, Saheed Adeyinka. "Neocolonialism." Encyclopedia of Postcolonial Studies. Ed. John C. Hawley. Westport: Greenwood, 2001.

Fanon, Fritz. "On National Culture." The Wretched of the Earth. New York: Grove, 1963. 206-48.

Feroza Jussawalla and Reed Way Dasenbrock Eds. Interviews with Writers of the Post-Colonial World. Jackson: UP of Mississippi, 1992. 25-41.

Ngugi wa Thiong'o. Weep Not, Child. African Writers Series. Oxford, Eng.: Heinemann, 1987.

Patke, Rajeev S. "Frantz Fanon (1925-1961)." Encyclopedia of Postcolonial Studies. Ed. John C. Hawley. Westport: Greenwood, 2001.

Vassanji, M.G. The In-Between World of Vikram Lall. New York: Knopf, 2004.

Chapter Seven
Trojan Alternatives

Note
1.Igbo (Eastern Nigeria) word for the 'ne'er do well' used here in its rather benign local context as against the opprobrium associated with its English equivalent.

Works Cited
African Studies Centre, ASC. Library dossier on author Mongo Beti from http://www.ascleiden.nl/Librar y/Webdossiers/Mong oBeti.aspx retrieved 21/09/05

Biakolo, A. "African Folklore and Anecdotes" CALEL Vol 2, No. 1 2004.

Haanel, C. The Master Key. Cheshire Psychology Publishing 1970.

Ce, C. "Bards and Tyrants: Literature, Leadership and Citizenship Issues of Modern Nigeria" African Literary Journal B5, 2005.

- - -. "Sail On" Full Moon and other Poems. Enugu Handel Books 2001

Drake, St. Clair "An Approach to the Evaluation of African Societies" Presence Africaine. Paris 1958.

Gakwandi, S. A. The Novel in Contemporary Africa. Nairobi Heinemann 1977. King, B. and Ogungbesan, K. Eds. A Celebration of Black and African Writing.Zaria: Ahmadu Bello University, 1975.

- - -. The New English Literatures. London: Macmillan 1980.

La Guerre, John ed. Calcutta to Caroni: The East Indians of Trinidad. London: Longman, 1974.

Logan, R. W. "The American Negro's View of Africa" Presence Africaine.Paris 1958.

Naipaul, V. S. A House for Mr Biswas. London: Penguin Books, 1961.

- - -. Miguel Street. London: Penguin Books, 1959.

- - -. The Mystic Masseur. London: Penguin Books, 1957.

Smythe, H. H. "The African Elite in Nigeria" Presence Africaine .Paris 1958.

Chapter Eight
Desolate Realities

Works Cited

Acheson, James. Samuel Beckett's Artistic Theory and Practice. New York: St.Martin's Press, 1997.

Acholonu, Catherine Obianuju. "A Touch of the Absurd: Soyinka and Beckett." African Literature Today 14. (1984): 12-18.

Adedeji, Joel. "Aesthetics of Soyinka's Theatre." Before Our Very Eyes. Ed. Dapo Adelugba. Ibadan: Spectrum Books Limited, 1987. 104-131.

Andres, Gunter. "Being Without Time" On Beckett's Play Waiting for Godot. Ed. Martin Esslin. Englewood Cliffs: Prentice Hall, 1965. 140-152.

Astro, Alan. Understanding Samuel Beckett. Colombia: Colombia University Press, 1990.

Beckett, Samuel. Waiting for Godot. London: Faber and Faber, 1965.

Bodkin, Maud. Archetypal Patterns in Poetry. London, Oxford, Glasgow: Oxford University Press, 1978.

Chinweizu, et al. Toward the Decolonisation of African Literature 1. Enugu: Fourth Dimension Publishing, 1980.

Cook, David. African Literature: A Critical View. London: Longman Group Ltd, 1977.

Fletcher, S. Beryl and John Fletcher. A Student Guide to the Plays of Samuel Beckett. London: Faber and Faber, 1985.

Gikandi, Simon. "Theory, Literature and Moral Considerations." Research in African Literature 32.4 (Winter 2001): 1-18.

Hegel, G.W.F. The Phenomenology of Mind. Trans. J.B. Baillie.George Allen and Unwin Ltd. New York: London and The Macmillan Company, 1931.

Hobson, Harold in Samuel Beckett: The Critical Heritage. Eds. Lawrence Gravner and Raymond Federman. London: Routledge and Kegan Paul, 1979.

Idowu, Bolaji E. African Traditional Religion: A Definition. Ibadan: Fountain Publications, 1991.

Jones, Edred Durosimi. The Writings of Wole Soyinka. London: Heinemann Educational Books Ltd, 1983.

Jung, Carl Gustav. Modern Man in Search of a Soul. Trans. W.S. Dell and Cary F. Baynes London: Routledge and Kegan Paul, 1966.

Kiberd, Declan. Inventing Ireland. Cambridge, Massachusetts: Harvard University Press, 1995.

Kierkegaard, Søren. "Attack Upon Christendom." A Kierkegaard Anthology. Ed. Robert Bretall. New York: Modern Library, 1946.

Kluckhohn, Clyde. "Recurrent Themes in Mythmaking." Myth and Mythmaking. Ed. Henry A. Murray. Boston: Beacon Press, 1968. 46-60.

Kojeve, Alexandre. Introduction to the Reading of Hegel. Lectures on the Phenomenology of Spirit. Ed. Alan Bloom. New York and London: Basic Books. Inc. Publishers.1969.

Kundert-Gibbs, John Leeland. No-Thing is Left to Tell: Zen/Chaos Theory in the Dramatic Art of Samuel Beckett. Madison, NJ: Fairleigh Dickenson University Press, 1999.

Mbiti, S. John. African Religions and Philosophy. London: Heinemann Educational Books Ltd., 1969.

Moore, Gerald. Wole Soyinka. London: Evans Brothers Ltd, 1971.Nietzsche, Friedrich, Wilhelm. The Portable Nietzsche. Ed. Walter Kaufmann. New York: Viking Press, 1954.

Ngezem, Eugene. "A Broken Compass: Modern Leadership in the Plays of Samuel Beckett and Harold Pinter." 25-26 Alizés (MaySeptember 2005): 110-127.

Sogolo, Godwin. Foundations of African Philosophy. Ibadan: Ibadan University Press, 1993.

Soyinka, Wole. The Swamp Dwellers in Three Short Plays. London: Oxford

University Press, 1983.

Webb, Eugene. The Plays of Samuel Beckett. Seattle: University of Washington Press, 1972.

Chapter Nine
The Existential Maturation

Notes

1.In one of the more illustrative instances of a critic misreading Disgrace as a result of Coetzee's deceivingly subtle prose, Martin Swales argues that "any attempt to read David's exploitation of the black population does not carry much conviction not least because Melanie is white" (9). However, as Gareth Cornwell notes, "[f]rom their physical descriptions and other clues, it would seem that both [Soraya and Melanie] are, in South African nomenclature, Coloreds" ("Realism" 315).

2 Michiel Heynes, Linda Seidel, Jacqueline Rose, Mike Kissack & ichael Titlestad, and Sue Kossew respectively.

3."Grace," it should be noted, is not the opposite of "disgrace," as both Derek Attridge and Charles Sarvan have observed in their discussions of Coetzee's novel. The concept of "grace," rather than appear as an antonym of "disgrace" alongside "honor" or "noble," implies beauty, refinement, or elegance.

4.In the spirit of morale-building, Cape Technical University allows adjunct instructors to teach one course a year in their respective fields of expertise.

5.Savran rightfully notes that the lack of desire Lurie experiences contains echoes of Buddhist doctrine, but erroneously assumes this marks an epiphany on David's part, a final rejection of earthly misery. He neglects to note Lurie's "pleasure in living has been snuffed out" by the experience, an emotion closer to the malaise which often accompanies the Schopenhauerean sublimation of the Will than to the sense of contentment Buddhists experience at the moment of release from earthly suffering.

Works Cited

Attridge, Derek. "Age of Bronze, State of Grace: Music and Dogs in Coetzee's Disgrace." Novel 34.1 (2000): 98-121.

Barnard, Rita. "J.M. Coetzee's Disgrace and the South African Pastoral." Contemporary Literature" Novel 44.2 (2003): 199-224.

Charles, Ron. "'A Morality Tale With No Easy Answers': With Disgrace, J.M. Coetzee Wins England's Booker Prize Again." The Christian Science Monitor (Boston) 10 November 1999: 20.

Coetzee, J.M. Disgrace. New York: Viking Penguin, 1999.

Cornwell, Gareth. "Realism, Rape, and J.M. Coetzee's Disgrace." Critique 43.4 (2002): 307-22.

---. "Disgraceland: History and the Humanities in Frontier Country." English in Africa 30.2 (2003): 43-59.

Gorra, Michael. "After the Fall." Rev. of Disgrace, by J.M. Coetzee. New York Times 28 Nov. 1999: BR7+.

Heynes, Michiel. "'Call No Man Happy': Perversity as Narrative Principle in Disgrace." English Studies in Africa 45.1 (2002): 57-65.

Hynes, James. "Sins of the Father." Rev. of Disgrace, by J.M. Coetzee. Washington Post 16 January 2000: X1+.

Kissack, Mike and Michael Titlestad. "Humility in a Godless World: Shame, Defiance and Dignity in Coetzee's Disgrace." Journal of Commonwealth Literature 38.3 (2003): 135-147.

Kossew, Sue. "The Politics of Shame and Redemption in J.M. Coetzee's Disgrace." Research in African Literatures 34.2 (2003): 155-62.

Rose, Jacqueline. "Apathy and Accountability: South Africa's Truth and Reconciliation Commission." Raritan 21.4 (2002): 175-95.

Savran, Charles. "Disgrace: A Path to Grace?" World Literature Today 78.1 (2004): 26-29.

Seidel, Linda. "Death and Transformation in J.M. Coetzee's Disgrace." Journal of Colonialism and Colonial History 2. 3 (2002). <http://muse.jhu.edu/journals/journal_of_colonialism_and_colonial _history/v002/2.3/seidel.html>. 3 April 2005.

Swales, Martin. "Sex, Shame and Guilt: Reflections on Bernhard Schlink's Der Vorleser (The Reader) and J.M. Coetzee's Disgrace." Journal of European Studies 33.1 (2003): 7-22.

Wicomb, Zoë. "Translations in the Yard of Africa." Journal of Literary Studies 18.3/4 (2002): 209-223.

Chapter Ten
African Modernity

Notes

1. Paul Gilroy, The Black Atlantic: Modernity and Double Consciousness (Cambridge, Mass: Harvard UP, 1993) 195.

2. Ihechukwu Madubuike, "Form, Structure, and Esthetics of the

Senegalese Novel," Journal of Black Studies 4.3 (March 1974): 346. 345-359.

3.Oscar Ronald Dathorne, The Black Mind: A History of African Literature (Minneapolis: University of Minnesota Press, 1974) 378.

4 .W.E.B. Du Bois, The Souls of Black Folk (New York: Gramercy 1994)

5.Vincent B. Khapoya, The African Experience: An Introduction (Upper Saddle River, NJ: Prentice Hall, 1998) 111; A. Adu Boahen, African Perspectives on Colonialism, (Baltimore: John Hopkins UP, 1989) 63.

6.Aime Cesaire, Discourse on Colonialism (New York, NY : Monthly Review Press, 2000) 42-43.

7. Khapoya, 120.

8. Michael Crowder, Senegal: A Study in French Assimilation Policy (New York: Oxford UP, 1962) 2.

9.Frantz Fanon. The Wretched of the Earth: Negro Psychoanalyst Study of the Problem of Racism & Colonialism in the World Today (New York: Grove Press, 1963) 124-125.

10.Madeleine Rousseau. "Crise de la culture noire," Présence Africaine, June- September (1957): 334.

11.Karen Thorsen's documentary The Price of the Ticket (1989), a posthumous video tribute to James Baldwin, has a scene in which poet Maya Angelou describes the surprise that many Black-American expatriate intellectuals such as Baldwin and Wright felt disillusioned when they realized that the French were racists toward Black people even if they acted as passionate devotee of "Negro" art. See Karen Thorsen, dir., James Baldwin: the Price of the Ticket (San Francisco, CA: California Newsreel, 1990).

12. Jacques Chevrier, Littérature Nègre: Afrique, Antilles, Madagascar (Paris: Armand Colin, 1974) 149.

Works Cited

Appiah, Kwame Anthony. In My Father's House: Africa in the Philosophy of Culture. New York and Oxford: Oxford UP. 1992.

Blair, Dorothy S. African Literature in French: A History of Creative Writing in French from West and Equatorial Africa. London: Cambridge UP. 1976.

Boahen, A. Adu. African Perspectives on Colonialism. Baltimore: John Hopkins UP. 1989.

Bonnett, Aubrey W and G. Llewellyn Watson. Emerging Perspectives on the Black Diaspora. Lanham, MD: UP of America. 1990.

Cesaire, Aime. Discourse on Colonialism. 1955. New York, NY : Monthly Review Press. 2000.

Chevrier, Jacques. Littérature Nègre: Afrique, Antilles, Madagascar. Paris: Armand Colin. 1974.

Chowdhury, Kanishka. "Afrocentric Voices: Constructing Identities, Displacing Difference." College Literature. West Chester. June 1997.

Crowder, Michael. Senegal: A Study in French Assimilation Policy. New York: Oxford UP. 1962.

Dathorne, Oscar Ronald. The Black Mind: A History of African Literature. Minneapolis: University of Minnesota Press. 1974. 378.Du Bois, W.E.B. The Souls of Black Folk. New York: Gramercy. 1994.

Fanon, Frantz. The Wretched of the Earth: Negro Psychoanalyst Study of the Problem of Racism & Colonialism in the World Today. New York: Grove Press. 1963

---, Black Skin White Masks: The Experiences of a Black Man in a White World. 1952. New York: Grove Press, Inc. 1967. Translated by Charles Lam Markman.

Feuser, Willfried, and Dathorne, O.R., Eds. Africa in Prose. Baltimore, MD: Penguin. 1969

Gilroy, Paul. The Black Atlantic: Modernity and Double Consciousness. Cambridge, Mass: Harvard UP. 1993

Harrow, Kenneth W. Faces of Islam in African Literature. London: Heinemann. 1991

Irele, F. Abiola. The African Imagination: Literature in Africa & the Black Diaspora. New York, NY: Oxford UP. 2001

Kane, Cheikh Hamidou. Ambiguous Adventure. 1962. Toronto: Macmillan. 1969

Kesteloot, Lilyan. Black Writers in French: A Literary History of Negritude. Philadelphia: Temple UP. 1974

Khapoya, Vincent B. The African Experience: An Introduction. 1994. Upper Saddle River, NJ: Prentice Hall. 1998.

Leeming, David. James Baldwin: A Biography. New York, NY: Alfred A. Knopf. 1994

Madubuike, Ihechukwu. The Senegalese Novel: A Sociological Study of the Impact of the Politics of Assimilation. Washington, D.C.: Three Continents Press.1983.

Nantet, Jacques. Panorama de la literature noire d'expression Francaise. Fayard: Les Grandes Etudes Littéraires. 1972

Rousseau, Madeleine. "Crise de la culture noire." Présence Africaine. June-September 1957.

Thorsen, Karen, dir. James Baldwin: The Price of the Ticket. San Francisco, CA : California Newsreel. 1990.

Walker, Keith L. Countermodernism and Francophone Literary Culture: The Game of Slipknot. Durham and London: Duke UP. 1999.

Counter Discourse

COUNTER Discourse charts the widening frontiers of black literary aesthetics using the prose and dramatic fictions of Anglophone, Lusophone and Francophone writers from Africa and the African Diaspora. The chapters come in two interactive phases of current critical discourses involving rejoinders from past-present concerns and issues of cultural and contemporary modernity. These studies stress the argument that African literature is hardly discussed outside contemporary history and that the reason for the apparent disconnection among groups in Africa and the Diaspora can be traced to the disparate elements within the continent and her Diaspora.

We expect that these series inaugurate a widening trend in African literary criticism that embraces formerly uncharted currents in the imaginative literatures of Africa and consistent with our collegiate vision of imaginatively 'reconstructing' African literature in a way that departs from old attitudes thereby crystallising in multi dimensional appreciation of her literary and cultural heritage.

.

African Library of Critical Writing

Liberian professor of African languages and literature, founder of the Society of African Folklore, and Literary Society International, LSi, Charles Smith, is editor of the Critical Writing Series on African Literature with Nigerian Chin Ce, books, news, reviews editor and research and creative writer. As one of the younger stream of poets from Africa, Ce is also the author of several works of fiction and essays on African and Caribbean literature.

Our Mission

African Books Network

AFRICAN Books Network with its cosmopolitan outlook is poised to meet the book needs of African generations in times to come. Since the year 2000 when we joined the highway of online solutions in publishing and distribution, our African alliance to global information development excels in spite of challenges in the region. Our select projects have given boost to the renaissance of a whole generation of dynamic literature. In our wake is the harvest of titles that have become important referrals in contemporary literary studies. With print issues followed by eContent and eBook versions, our network has demonstrated its commitment to the vision of a continent bound to a common heritage. This universal publishing outlook is further evidenced by our participation in African Literature Research projects. For everyone on deck, a hands-on interactive is the deal which continues to translate to more flexibility in line with global trends ensuring that African writers are part of the information gobalisation of the present.

As one of Africa's mainstream book publishing and distribution networks, many authors may look to us for to privileged assistance regarding affiliate international and local publishing and distribution service

"Our select projects at African Books Network have given boost to the renaissance of a whole generation of dynamic literature."